CW00501004

My Life on the Line

Also by Simon Rae

Non-fiction
W.G. Grace: A Life
It's Not Cricket

Fiction – Inspector Dalliance series
Bodyline
The Pill Box Murders
Hangman

My Life on
the Line

Everything you didn't know
you needed to know about
being an assistant referee

by Gavin Muge
with Simon Rae

NINE
ELMS

Published in 2022 by
Nine Elms Books Ltd
Unit 6b, Clapham North Arts Centre
26-32 Voltaire Road,
London SW4 6DH
info@nineelmsbooks.co.uk
www.nineelmsbooks.co.uk

ISBN print 978-1-910533-67-3
ISBN e-book 978-1-910533-68-0

Copyright © 2022 Gavin Muge and Simon Rae

Protected by copyright under the terms of the International Copyright
Union. The rights of Gavin Muge and Simon Rae Nicholas to be identified as
the authors of this work have been asserted by them in accordance with the
Copyright, Designs and Patents Act, 1988. All rights reserved.

This book is sold under the condition that no part of it may be reproduced,
copied, stored in a retrieval system or transmitted in any form or by any
means, electronic, mechanical, photocopying, recording or otherwise
without prior – permission of the author.

Every effort has been made to contact all copyright holders. The publishers
will be pleased to amend in future editions any errors or omissions brought
to their attention.

Cover illustration. design, typesetting and layout by
Alan Cooper Design *www.alancooperdesign.co.uk*

Printed and bound in the UK by Clays Ltd, Suffolk NR35 1ED
www.clays.co.uk

To my friends, fellow match officials,
everyone who loves the game
and Jacqueline.

CONTENTS

My job on the line.
(Northampton Town v Scunthorpe United, EFL League 1. January 2017.)

INTRODUCTION

My Life on the Line is unique. Counter-intuitively, it's a book about someone you've never heard of, whose role in the world's most popular sport is to remain almost totally anonymous, though the decisions he/she makes are vehemently criticised by thousands of fanatical 'experts', watching their every move. Literally millions of pounds can rest on their split-second judgments, yet they shoulder their responsibilities for relatively modest rewards. Who on earth would want to be an assistant referee – or 'lino' in old money?

Gavin Muge, for one. Gavin is a football fan through and through and a life-long Luton supporter (as was Eric Morecambe). From watching the Hatters as a young boy, he started to play the game and, like numberless thousands of kids, wanted to follow his heroes and grow up to be a star. When he realised he wasn't going to be good enough, he experimented with refereeing at youth level, later making the commitment required to reach the National List of Assistant Referees.

Gavin is a meticulous archivist and could tell you about every single one of the 250+ Football League matches he officiated in during his nine seasons on the Football League line. Happily, he isn't going to do that in this book, having teamed up with Simon Rae, who, as a result of researching his definitive biography of the world's greatest cricketer, W. G. Grace, is now allergic to all sports statistics, records, match results, players' names and anything else he might be expected to remember.

Instead, Gavin will tell you about what it is actually like being that close to the action in professional football; how crowds react to your decisions; what the players are like; what managers are like; what the whole match-day experience is like. Once characterised by a colleague at work as his 'hobby', Gavin can assure you that running the line is a lot more demanding and exciting than trainspotting – especially when things get feisty. A case in point is the Riot of Upton Park (August 2009), when Gavin was the linesman in a Cup tie between rivals West Ham and Millwall. He was at the end of the ground where the West Ham supporters spent much of the evening trying to start a battle with Millwall supporters, hurling seats at stewards and ending up invading the pitch.

He'll also run through how you get to those heights. And it's not a question of having the right kit and a passable understanding of the offside rule. In fact, you'll learn more than you ever knew you needed to know about being a match official, including the answers to questions like: 'How many shirts does an assistant referee take with them on match days?' and 'How much does a linesman's flag cost?'

A thread of personal memories, insights and opinions runs through the book, with Gavin giving an informed view of all aspects of the game, including travelling the length of England and Europe as a fan in the 80s and 90s, the era of the terrible disasters of Heysel and Hillsborough, along with constant trouble at home and abroad. In Sweden, he evaded a mounted police charge, preferring to take sanctuary with a local girl he'd met in the crowd before the match. He'll also give a professional view of those controversial decisions – that 'goal' in the 1966 World Cup final, Maradona's 'Hand of God' goal twenty years later, and Frank Lampard's disallowed goal in 2010, along with many other classic controversies, culminating in an assessment of VAR, plus provocative thoughts on how the Laws of the Game could be changed to improve it for the faithful millions who devote so much time, money and passion to supporting their teams.

The book also gives a brief history of the game, from its rough and riotous origins as a form of mass community warfare to the global phenomenon it is today. And as *My Life on the Line* is published in World Cup year, there'll be a focus on the world's biggest football event.

My Life on the Line has something for everyone interested in the beautiful game, including entertainment for those who like a challenge. Gavin's Quiz will get you scratching your head with questions like: 'What is taken to the FA Cup final every year and never used?' and 'Which club has held the Cup for the longest period?' The middle chapters are bookended by 'Chapter Challenges' – conundrums drawn from the multiplicity of unlikely things that happen all the time in the world's most popular sport.

My Life on the Line is a Swiss Army knife of a book – one to take on the supporters' bus or read on the train; or to keep by the bed to soothe you to sleep when relegation anxieties produce a firestorm of insomnia. You'll be able to impress your friends with your new-found knowledge and make yourself an irreplaceable member of your pub quiz team.

PART 1

A FOOTBALL
SELF-PORTRAIT

CHAPTER 1

Hatters' Tea Party

Me, Eric Morecambe and a Lifelong Commitment to Luton Town FC

Two tiny football boots dangling from the hood of my pram. How did Mum know? Would my life have been different if a pair of boxing gloves had caught her eye instead? It doesn't matter now. The die is cast. Intended as a distraction as she pushed me around the shops, those boots turned out to be a life script.

I was born in Harpenden in 1969, and that meant (according to my uncle) that as a football fan, I would either go 'Left for Luton or Right for Watford'. I chose Left for Luton and thus became a Hatter (because of the town's historic association with hat-making). Like most football clubs, Luton has had an up-and-down history. Okay, more down than up, but in the mid-seventies the club was riding high, enjoying playing in the top flight (the old Division 1). In 1974, the players teamed up with comedy band The Barron Knights to produce a rousing Club song, 'Hatters, Hatters'. This may not have gone platinum, but it

CHAPTER CHALLENGES

1. *How old do you need to be to be an FA qualified referee?*

2. *How old do you need to be to play official 11v11 football?*

is a sterling celebration of the Luton ethos and can be enjoyed to this day on YouTube. It even has a special reference to the club's 'number-one fan', Eric Morecambe, 'wiggling' his glasses and sharing that world-famous smile.

Eric Morecambe had moved south from the seaside resort that gave him his stage name to take up residence at Harpenden in the sixties. A keen football fan, he faced the coin toss – Luton or Watford – and, appropriately, given his propensity for slightly Alice in Wonderland humour, became a Hatter. In due course, he joined the board of the club while his fellow entertainer, Elton John, was chairman of rivals Watford.

Soon out of my pram, my first conscious desire was for a football. Second only to a guitar or drumkit, this is the present most immediately regretted by doting parents. The taps against the wall, the headers over the garden fence, the glancing blow to the car in the drive, the slick of dog muck after a kick-about on the Green opposite our house: a never-ending source of tension, apprehension, recrimination, pleading and sullen apology. But for all the upsets, my football was undoubtedly the most important thing in my life.

The cartoon catalogue of catastrophe culminated in a visit to my grandparents one Sunday afternoon. The grown-ups were intent, as always, on talking endlessly about neighbours, friends and a couple of politicians called Mr Heath and Mr Wilson, leaving four-year-old me to entertain myself in the garden, with all the usual warnings against kicking my ball too hard, too high, too far.

What could possibly go wrong?

I dribbled around the bench; I dummied the plum tree; I left the water feature for dead and, in a final burst of world-beating exuberance, smashed the ball top bins – oh! – oh no!! – oh dear! – through a window in the greenhouse.

I trotted up just to make sure…but no, it wasn't an optical illusion. There was the broken pane, with its venomous splinters spreading over the floor, and there was my football, nestling in the ruins of one of Grandpa's prize-winning tomato plants. I could see concocting a story that got me off the hook for this act of vandalism was going to take some quick thinking.

But I ran out of time. The telling tinkle had already sounded the alarm and the inevitable posse of grown-ups poured out into the garden to inspect the damage. Mum did that thing that mums are so good at – telling me off while apologising to the victims of my latest outrage at the same time. Grandpa tried to pour oil on troubled water, saying he'd have it cleared up in a jiffy, would replace the pane of glass in the morning, and could probably save the tomato plant into the bargain. He then strode into the greenhouse and nearly sliced a finger off picking up the first razor-sharp shard.

My plaintive 'Can I have my ball back?' fell on deaf ears, and I was hauled off to the car – more Dennis the Menace than Denis Law – roundly condemned for ruining the whole day.

Possibly in an attempt to ween me off my dangerous obsession with football, I was given a brand-new Raleigh Tomahawk for my sixth birthday. But I didn't want it. So I didn't ride it. In fact, I asked Mum to sell it and buy me something more useful, i.e. a set of goal posts instead. Which she did; and when they were set up, I played and played and played.

Obviously, there came a time when I was called in for some chore like eating my tea or getting ready for bed. And there were days when it was wet or cold and I couldn't play outside. But football could still be played indoors.

Subbuteo was becoming increasingly popular, with its wobbly players that you flicked around the pitch. But I had Striker, which was better – 'Players actually kick the ball', as it said on the box. You pressed the head of the players down to make their legs move, and they would actually 'kick' the ball. Fantastic.

For my eighth birthday, Mum baked me a special football pitch cake. It was lovely and green but, while she had got white icing for the lines, she'd marked out a netball court rather than a football pitch. Stickler for accuracy in all things as I already was, I made her do the markings again.

But she scored an absolute worldy for my next birthday: my first football boots – a Kevin Keegan pair, which had real screw-in studs that gave me endless hours of fun tightening and retightening them. (I took them out altogether at bedtime when I went to sleep still wearing the boots.)

In 1977, I started at Wood End Junior School in Harpenden. My class teacher, Miss Cartmel, wrote in my first report: 'Football is very interesting, but not for *every* story.' Well, it's a point of view. At an early parents' evening, Miss Cartmel gave Mum a present for me – a set of red/yellow cards that she'd made as a form of encouragement to work hard at school. Clearly another pointer to the life ahead.

On 21st March 1978, I saw my first ever game. My Uncle Adrian took me. It was Luton Town v Bolton Wanderers. I was star-struck as I marched proudly into the ground, knocked out by the floodlights, the snooker-table sward of the pitch, the tidal waves of cheers and chants from the crowd, the smell of cooked onions – the whole unmistakable atmosphere of our great game. Despite the array of talent in the Bolton team, including Peter Reid and Sam Allardyce, Luton clinched victory 2-1, and I shouted myself hoarse with happiness.

I was so mesmerised by the whole experience, I wanted to become a part of it. I wrote to the club asking if I could be one of the ball boys, scurrying up and down the touchline, throwing the ball back when it got kicked into touch. Sadly, the answer was no, but they sent me details of the Junior Hatters club, along with signed photos from Jake Findlay and Kirk Stephens. I joined straight away.

The following year, 1979, I made history. At least, I think I did. I played for Wood End Junior School while in the second year, aged nine. Normally, you had to wait until you were a fourth year, aged 11. As far as I knew, no one had done it before me, and if that isn't history, I don't know what is. In the same year, I repeated history by smashing something with a football. I had my brother to blame this time. We were playing headers in the front room, and Mum came in to find her favourite Beatrix Potter Tom Kitten figurine smashed to smithereens in the ceramic surround to the electric fire. She was not mollified by our strenuous attempts to blame each other.

1980 saw me succumb to a bizarre moment of over-ambition when I joined a couple of friends to form the editorial team of a school football newspaper. Everybody loved football, so, we reckoned, we had a captive readership, and set to filling a couple of sheets of A4 with commentary on the previous Saturday's fixtures. These we photocopied and stapled together before taking them into school and distributing them among our friends.

One problem. The paper was over a week old by the time we had copies to share, and one definition of news is 'something I didn't know before you told me'. We weren't telling anybody anything they didn't know already, and the sceptical reception our paper got was an instant downer. My faith in the project took a final plunge when I saw some of my friends dancing around the playground wearing their copies as party hats. We hadn't even done the stapling properly, so the two sheets rapidly separated and soon fluttered off to roost on the roof of the bike shed. That one edition was all we managed, and my fantasy of becoming a sports journalist and getting a free pass into any football match I wanted to see withered on the vine.

Of course, being a football writer was a poor second to becoming a professional footballer. That was still my burning ambition. And in the 1980/81 season, I took a step towards realising that dream by playing for Harpenden Colts as a nippy winger. I ran up and down the right wing like crazy, yelling for the ball and launching crosses and shots whenever I had the chance. You couldn't fault me for dedication and effort, but even at that young age, I wasn't blind to the fact that there were plenty of other lads who could play a bit – some of them a bit better than me.

But although I wouldn't bet the bank on my playing for England, I wasn't going to let anything get in the way of supporting the Three Lions, especially in a World Cup Year. 1982 saw Spain hosting, and England, under Ron Greenwood, had made it through to the finals, which fell in late June/early July. This was when we usually took our summer holiday. Dad worked for a local car dealer, so had to be back in August when the new registration plates were issued. In those days, there wasn't a problem with taking children out of school to fall in with family holiday plans.

But if school was okay with our going away in June, I wasn't. I couldn't believe my parents hadn't checked the FIFA calendar before booking the holiday. They could go to France if they wanted to, but I was staying put. I was in secondary school by now, and reluctantly Mum agreed I could stay with a friend of hers. There can't be many instances of someone voluntarily staying in school instead of going on holiday, but I did without hesitation simply so I could watch the England team.

They did surprisingly well, given that both Trevor Brooking and Kevin Keegan weren't fit enough to play in the first group games. Eventually, England had to beat Spain by two goals to get to the semi-finals. Both stars came on for the last 20 minutes, and both had chances – Keegan's a simple header into the net – but they both missed. So England were out – without losing a single match and only conceding one goal.

It was agonising – but good preparation for the years of disappointment ahead. Not that I knew that then. 1982 was the first World Cup finals England had made in 12 years, and naturally I thought we'd be there next time, pushing for a place in the final. I certainly wouldn't have missed it for the world – or at least, not for a two-week holiday in France.

The new season was an exciting prospect. Luton had been promoted, and their fans could look forward to rubbing shoulders with the elite in Division 1, as it was in those days. Kenilworth Road would host all of them, making every other Saturday something to look forward to. But there was something else I really wanted to experience: my first away game. I didn't mind who it was against. I just wanted to feel the vibe of one of the really big stadiums and be part of the outnumbered but unintimidated cohort of travelling Hatters. Dad promised to fix it. He knew most of the Luton players and said he'd be able to get tickets from somebody.

> " England were out – without losing a single match and only conceding one goal.

A Friday night in early September. I waited at my Nan's house for Dad to collect me. Tomorrow looked like an amalgamation of Christmas and my birthday with an amazing present awaiting me. But was it going to happen? The smile on his face when he walked into the sitting room answered that. Yes, he'd got the tickets and yes, we were actually going to Anfield!

Did I sleep that night? Did I heck. I lay in the dark playing all the possibilities of the match over and over again in my head, trying to think positive thoughts about Luton's chances against the country's dominant team, the reigning champions, the legendary Reds.

Dad drove me and a school friend, Steve, up the M1 and M6 with orange scarves proudly fluttering from the car windows. It was a lovely sunny day and the trip whizzed by. We passed a few supporters' coaches and fellow Luton fans waved and gave us the thumbs up as soon as they saw our colours. There was a great feeling of togetherness, of being part of a great adventure.

The M6 became the M62, and as we reached the junction with Queens

Drive, we saw the reception committee – a car full of locals driving up and down 'waving' at any obvious Bedfordshire tourists. We had pulled the scarves in by this stage, so passed on by without attracting attention.

We could tell we were getting closer to Anfield. It was like any football ground on match day – the purposeful crowds on the pavements spilling out into the road, the gathering noise of cheers and chants, supporters' coaches inching their way forwards. And we were a tiny part of it all.

Parking became imperative, and Dad found a spot. As he drew up alongside the curb, a local lad skidded to a halt on his bike and offered to 'Look after your car, Mister?' Price – a fiver. Dad handed over the money and we all hopped out and joined the throng.

Anfield at last, and it looked majestic! Hundreds of supporters milling about and an electric atmosphere. Dad collected the tickets, left for us by Luton star David Moss, and we took our seats in the main stand. At this point, I became aware of lots of people staring at me. My white Luton shirt stood out a bit among the sea of red.

But at 12, I was excused – too young to know better, and clearly no threat to any of the home supporters. In fact, we received a warm Scouse welcome, with people near us telling their stories and engaging in a bit of banter about the likely outcome of the match. I was in football heaven. The pitch below us glowed green and the sky above was blue. But I focused mainly on the Kop – a magnificent sight, filled with Liverpool fans with their banners and their famous song list. Perfect.

The Luton team took the field first and I, along with 3,000 Hatters in the away section, gave them a big welcome.

Then the men in red appeared to thunderous applause... I looked at the superstars I'd only ever seen on TV before: Souness, Dalglish, Rush, Grobbelaar, Lawrenson, Whelan and the others all looked like the Champions they were.

I whispered to my dad, 'Do you think we're going to win?' He didn't answer and just gave me a knowing look. Maybe.

Well, we didn't win, but it was an amazing game that ended 3-3 – a remarkable achievement for the Hatters. It also had a rare feature: we had to use three different goalkeepers. Our number one, Jake Findlay, was injured in the first half, to be replaced by Kirk Stephens. That was changed at half time when Mal Donaghy went in goal. Both Kirk and Mal wore a Liverpool goalie top as Jake couldn't take his off due to his injury, and each of the three let in a goal. Almost certainly a first for the top flight of English football! With goals going in regularly at either end of the ground, it was a classic.

Final whistle and honours even. Time for home. Once we'd left the ground, my white shirt stood out like a cue ball as we walked along, and the Luton fans waiting patiently on the staircase overlooking Anfield Road gave me a wave and a song.

Back to the car and happily it hadn't been molested. A fiver well spent. The journey home was a joyful one, and we got back around 10pm. As a first away game, it was pretty special, and I hoped they would all be like that in future. In reality, that was not going to happen – not against the top clubs. The following February, Liverpool came to Luton, and this time there was no doubt which was the superior side, the Reds winning 3-1 on their way to another season as Champions.

Luton at least stayed up in Division 1 thanks to a memorable last day of the season victory at Manchester City. Along with my dad, brother and 5,000 other Hatters, I was there at the game and when Raddy Antić scored in the 86th minute to give us a 1-0 lead, the remaining time just couldn't go fast enough. Joy at the final whistle for Luton, but utter despair for Manchester City, who were relegated to Division 2 as a result of that game. How things have changed…

The following season, in October 1983, in a state of inflated optimism, we again went to Anfield. Again, there were six goals in the game. This time though, Ian Rush scored five and Kenny Dalglish got the other one to complete a 6-0 thrashing!

Meanwhile, my own progress towards the professional game was seriously handicapped by my secondary school. St George's was a good school. But there was one serious flaw – it didn't play football; it played rugby. Could this have been anything to do with the fact that the head of PE was Mr Rees from Wales? I couldn't possibly say. But I still associate a strong Welsh accent with the horror of those PE lessons when I was 11 and 12 and wanted to be sprinting down the touchline with the ball at my feet, rather than being crushed at the bottom of a scrum.

Another sport I wasn't keen on was cricket. But on one occasion, I actually begged to be allowed to play. 19th May 1984 anyone? That's right: the FA Cup final. And the finalists were Everton and Watford. As a Luton fan, this was a game to avoid. Not only were our rivals, Watford, an enviably good team with players like John Barnes, Luther Blissett, Kenny Jackett and Nigel Callaghan, but they had beaten Luton in our local derby in the third round – after a replay. Though the FA Cup final was the highlight of the season, I just couldn't bring myself to watch it. And yet I knew I couldn't stick around at home ignoring it. I'd have to know the score.

Hence my pleas to be allowed to play cricket for the school. Mr Rees was surprised, to put it mildly; but I knew what I was doing: no mobile phones in those days, and it was fairly easy to avoid the radio while standing in the long grass out on the boundary wondering how on earth anyone had invented such a terminally tedious game.

Even the longest day comes to an end, and I eventually returned to the real world to discover that Everton had triumphed 2-0. What a relief. And when I saw the goals, I could hardly believe the second one scored by Andy Gray. He more or less headed the ball right out of Steve Sherwood's hands. *Schadenfreude* doesn't come much sweeter than that!

CHAPTER CHALLENGES ANSWERS

1. *You need to be a minimum of 14 years old to be a trainee referee with the FA.*

2. *11v11 football begins at Under-13 level. If the age bracket is 11-13, then an 11-year-old can play.*

CHAPTER 2

Playing Peak

Me, Gary Lineker and the Player of the Year Award

The photograph shows us both as much (much) younger. This is no surprise, as it was taken in May 1985, when Gary was the established England striker and I was a gawky teenager full of ambition to emulate him. On that particular day, my confidence was high.

After all, I had a cup to authenticate it. The meeting took place in the Chiltern Hotel, Luton, and I was there to collect my Under-15 Player of the Year Award. Gary, along with other England stalwarts Kenny Sansom, Peter Reid, Gary Stevens and Paul Bracewell, were there prior to their flight out to Finland the next day for a World Cup qualifying match. Giving a moment to pose for a photo with a young fan must have been run-of-the-mill for Gary, and I'm pretty sure the encounter stands taller in my memory than in his (England stats: 80 caps, 48 goals); but for that magic moment, I was mixing with the stars, dreaming it would only be a matter of time before I found my place among them.

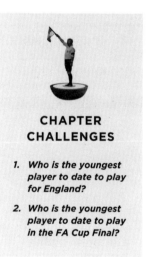

CHAPTER CHALLENGES

1. *Who is the youngest player to date to play for England?*

2. *Who is the youngest player to date to play in the FA Cup Final?*

Even at the time, for all my burning ambition, a reality check suggested that abundant enthusiasm probably wasn't enough. I had already developed a Plan B, based on the obvious fact that one guaranteed way of getting involved in football was to become a match official. The previous autumn, I had signed up for a Laws of Association Football instruction course at a local school and had passed both the eye test and the Laws of the Game exam. I was, in fact, qualified as a 'youth class referee'.

I doubt that came up in conversation with Gary. He was in the early stage of his career, so the topic of his professional life's freedom from any card, yellow or red, which is one of the standard facts everyone now knows about him, was not then a thing. And I don't suppose I was dishing out many cards as I ran around refereeing U11 and U12 matches in the Chiltern Youth League on Sunday mornings. Then – as now – it was probably over-exuberant parents who gave me the most trouble, especially as I would have looked barely older than the boys I was supervising. Did we have the 'Respect' tapes fluttering in those days? Definitely not. But then – as now – there's no challenging the conviction that watching a million hours of professional football, live or on the telly, entitles you to slag off the decisions of a qualified match official. Then – as now – I did my best to ignore the jeers and abuse and get on with getting the next decision right.

> **The memory of my first experience of Wembley will live with me for the rest of my life.**

1985 was a transitional year. I was a dedicated follower of Luton by now – my tally for the 85/86 season was 37 games, 24 home, 13 away. I also went to Wembley for the first time, to see Everton beat Manchester United 2-0 in the Charity Shield. This was the 'old Wembley', with its twin towers and raked stands (before it became an all-seater stadium in 1990). I was overawed by this most iconic of venues, with its long history of extraordinary matches, culminating in England's epic victory over the Germans in the World Cup final, 1966. I'm not making any great claims for the 1985 Charity Shield match, but the memory of my first experience of Wembley will live with me for the rest of my life.

With my Saturdays taken up with the more humdrum attendance at the Hatters' home matches, and refereeing Youth League football on Sundays (mornings and afternoons), there was less and less time for me to actually play the game. In addition, it was my O Levels year, and I was determined to do well – against parental expectations. Unsurprisingly, as they still had to do all the driving, Mum and Dad saw more of the football addict than the hard-working student as they ferried me from one game to the next.

But all went well: exams passed, Sixth Form place secured, and – another step towards the grown-up world – my first steady relationship. And on the football front, I made the step up to becoming a Class 3 referee. The grading system in those days was 3, 2, 1, and to get promoted you had to apply to the County FA to be assessed over three games, and to pass the fitness test (which a lot of the angry dads yelling at me every weekend would not have been able to do). Once you reached Class 1 status, you could then be promoted through the non-League system to the professional game.

I guess there was something in my psychological make-up that made an ordered progression to an achievable outcome attractive. It was more predictable than the lottery of trying to make it as a player. To climb the ladder as a referee, you were really only competing with yourself, whereas young players were involved in a tormenting lottery of catching the right person's eye, putting in a dazzling performance on the day of the trial match, and waiting – often in vain – for the all-important letter or phone call.

Refereeing – or running the line – kept you involved in the game. You were totally immersed in the whole match. You didn't experience the extreme high of scoring the winning goal; but nor did you suffer the low of missing a crucial tackle or shanking the ball over the crossbar from close range. Of course, you made mistakes, for which you would be roundly condemned by the spectators, but you knew what you were doing and had the satisfaction of delivering as fair a match as possible. You were always on the pitch for the full 90 minutes. And you went home with a little bit of pocket money for your pains. It seemed a pretty good deal to me.

In 1986, I was linesman in an Under-12 cup final, and the following May, I was referee for an Under-11 cup final. By this time, I was driving myself to the ground. I had my passport to the adult world, a driving licence. I celebrated by cramming some mates into my green Vauxhall Viva and driving all the way up to Goodison Park to watch Luton play Everton in the last game of the season. It was a long haul at a sedate 60 mph, but we were in high spirits, celebrating our newly found freedom.

Parking on match days is always a challenge, and I managed to clip another vehicle as I squeezed into a tight space. Liverpool is not a city where you want to go damaging the locals' vehicles, but after a team inspection we reckoned we'd get away with it and slipped into the surging crowd queuing for the turnstiles.

Everton won the match 3-1. As it was also the day they were presented with the Division 1 trophy, it was quite a party. But we were definitely not invited. Visiting fans are usually kept in their places while the home crowd disperse. But not on this occasion. We were told in no uncertain terms that we were leaving first, and quickly. The police were probably anticipating a lively evening on Merseyside, and we were a complication they didn't need. I had hoped to see the presentation, but it was not to be. We drove back down the motorway disappointed at the result but feeling we'd had a brush with history.

That marked the start of my career as an independent football supporter, and in 1987/88, Luton gave their fans a lot to get excited about. They reached the Simod Cup final but lost to Reading 1-4. They reached the FA Cup semi-final but lost 1-2 to Wimbledon, who went on to inflict a shattering defeat on favourites Liverpool in the final. But Luton had some giant-killing of their own to perform. They reached the Football League Cup final (aka the

Littlewoods Challenge Cup final) against the holders and strongly fancied favourites, Arsenal.

With a car full of mates from school, I made a memorable journey to Oxford for the semi-final, driving down from Harpenden in heavy snow on a freezing February evening. Parking was a nightmare, so I followed others in abandoning the car on a roundabout close to the ground, which was packed – above the official capacity and beyond the powers of the police to control. After the match ended, there was a bottleneck at the away end, with an alleyway filled with supporters pushing to escape. The fence beside us simply gave way under the weight of bodies – many ending up pitched into the back gardens of the residents who lived next to the stadium. I doubt many were injured – it certainly wasn't Heysel. But it was a reminder that the lessons of Heysel still hadn't been learned.

The final at Wembley in April 1988 was the usual sell-out with a lot of pressure on ticket allocation. Arsenal were confident of repeating their success of the previous season, but they were startled by an early goal by Brian Stein, and the Hatters held the lead until half time. Arsenal pressure told and eventually they equalised, and then scored a second goal to take the lead. To make matters worse, they were then awarded a dubious penalty. For a reason I still can't fathom, Nigel Winterburn took the kick – and it was brilliantly saved by Andy Dibble. That gave us the momentum we needed to get back in the game and we equalised with a goal from Danny Wilson. Arsenal defender Gus Caesar was at fault, and I imagine the moment haunts him to this day.

In the 90th minute, we snatched victory with a glorious winner from Brian Stein – again – to make it 3-2. We had won our first major trophy, and this time there was no question of anyone leaving before we'd seen Steve Foster lead the team up the Wembley steps to receive the cup. And as he lifted it above his head, I and 30,000 other happy Hatters cheered loud and long. One of the unforgettable highs of a life dedicated to the game.

The next day, there was the traditional open-top bus tour through the town. Along with a bunch of pals, I nipped away from school the minute the bell went and took the train to Luton. We bagged a vantage point on the roof of the Arndale Shopping Centre, where we had a fabulous view of the players raising the cup again – this time from the Town Hall balcony. It was Hatters' heaven!

Back on earth, I kept up my refereeing with the Chiltern Youth League. On one occasion, I tried refereeing an adult game. This was in the Bedfordshire County Cup, and I didn't enjoy it all. I was a 17-year-old asked to control young men in their twenties. They were aggressive and intimidating, contesting my decisions and undermining my confidence. It was a horrible experience, and I gladly returned to youth football.

In the autumn of 1987, I was once again drawn into the adult world by an invitation to be the linesman in a warm-up game at Luton prior to a big First Division match versus Liverpool. I was also invited to Bisham Abbey to run the line in a friendly between Northern Ireland and Luton in November that year. There would have been a lot of people qualified for those two games, so I was obviously doing something right to get the nod.

My season – and indeed my sporting career – had taken a serious knock in October 1987 when I suffered an injury to my left knee. The medics had a go at fixing it, but hadn't succeeded, so I was down for an arthroscopy operation in December (Happy Christmas!) Like so many craving a professional life in sport (I had planned to go to university and train as a PE teacher), my hopes were scuppered by injury.

The 1988/89 season seemed normal. I refereed junior games and followed Luton home and away. The Hatters were doing well and even reached the Littlewoods League Cup final again, losing 3-1 to Nottingham Forest. Brian Clough's feisty mavericks also performed well in the FA Cup, and on 15th April 1989 met rivals Liverpool for a semi-final at the Hillsborough Stadium, Sheffield.

The events of that day will always be remembered as the Hillsborough Disaster, which ultimately cost 97 Liverpool fans their lives due to abjectly inadequate policing. The match commander, David Duckenfield, ordered Exit Gate C to be opened, causing the standing-only pens at the Leppings Lane end to flood with late-arrivals, producing a fatal crush which killed 94 on the day along with 766 injured. The scandal of the police cover-up, the disgraceful slurs of *The Sun* newspaper – which blamed the Liverpool supporters for the tragedy (even accusing the survivors of robbing the still warm bodies of their fellow fans) – and the succession of botched inquiries that ground on fruitlessly for decades mark the occasion as the darkest day in British sport.

Although the match was not screened live, the TV cameras were there, and the disaster was given rolling news coverage. The whole country was shocked by the scenes of fans being crushed against the fences, begging for help, passing kids out over the heads of adults who were themselves doomed. The haunting images will never be forgotten. It touched the hearts of every genuine football fan, and despite the smears of the gutter press, the nation mourned with a united Merseyside, whose red and blue scarfs carpeted Anfield in communal remembrance.

I just knew I had to make the pilgrimage myself, so set off with my friend Ben the following Saturday to register solidarity by laying flowers on a pitch strewn with thousands of other tributes. Anfield has always been an awesome stadium, but in the aftermath of Hillsborough it became a shrine for football fans from all over the UK – and beyond.

CHAPTER CHALLENGES ANSWERS

1. *Theo Walcott – aged 17 years and 75 days v Hungary in May 2006.*

2. *Curtis Weston – aged 17 years and 119 days in 2004 for Millwall v Manchester United.*

CHAPTER 3

Pitch Battles

Me, Millwall the Way It Was Then

I was venturing into 'beyond' myself. Later in 1989, I flew to America and worked as a summer camp counsellor at Camp Eagle Cove in Upstate New York coaching kids from 8 to 18. This was a brilliant experience. As people often say, when you arrive in the States, it feels like you've walked into a Hollywood movie. Everything is so big, so brash, so jaw-droppingly *American*! And an Englishman, shy and softly spoken, with *that* accent, was just as exotic to the locals.

I acclimatised quite quickly. After all, I was on home ground coaching (although I never really got used to everyone talking about 'soccer'), and it goes without saying I loved the US: the enormous cars, the five-lane motorways; the neon eye-candy enticing you to this diner, that drive-in cinema, and doubtless a few less savoury establishments – though teenagers were not allowed to buy a beer (while deemed responsible enough to own a gun!). Then there was the food: pizzas as

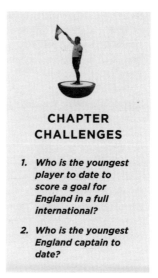

CHAPTER CHALLENGES

1. *Who is the youngest player to date to score a goal for England in a full international?*

2. *Who is the youngest England captain to date?*

big as a darts board, steaks the dimensions of a skateboard, breakfasts that would last you a week – and everything presented with pizzaz, reflecting the American temperament – exuberantly positive, can-do. It made a glorious contrast to life back home in Mrs Thatcher's Britain.

The 1980s had not been a good decade for the UK. The war against the Argentinians over the Falklands and the battles with the 'Enemy Within' (i.e. the striking miners under the leadership of Arthur Scargill) had resulted in much economic damage, with industries and businesses shutting down and unemployment figures high. This bred understandable bitterness and a toxic mix of defeatism and defiance, often expressed on the football terraces. Disaffected youth – or 'Rampaging Thugs' as the headlines had it – began to claim increasing front page coverage.

This was nothing new. Football had long been associated with violence from its days as a riotous public sport involving numberless combatants brawling through the streets of villages and towns to mark religious holidays. Even as the game established itself in its rules-based format in the second half of the Victorian period, matches were still targets for 'roughs' who welcomed the chance of a bit of recreational violence. This carried over into the 20th century, with the Old Firm encounters between Celtic and Rangers creating a steady stream of violent – and occasionally fatal – episodes.

As more and more fans took to the railways to follow their teams, there was a steady increase in vandalism to carriages and stations. In the mid-1950s, Liverpool and Everton supporters damaged several trains, and Everton's Goodison Park had a reputation for being one of the most hostile grounds to visit, with, according to one journalist, the 'roughest, rowdiest rabble' in the country.

Recorded incidents of hooliganism increased steadily throughout the sixties, along with the rise of unabashed and unreprimanded racism on a colossal scale as more black players established themselves in the game. Racism was even more prominent in the seventies, a decade which also saw the emergence of organised football gangs. These were known as firms or crews, and the craze spread with alarming speed: Leeds Service Crew (Leeds United), Red Army (Manchester United), The Gooners (Arsenal), Gremlins (Newcastle United), Blades Business Crew (Sheffield United), Suicide Squad (Burnley), Headhunters (Chelsea) and, most notorious of them all, Inter City Firm (West Ham United), though they were pushed hard by their hated local rivals, the Millwall Bushwackers. (We'll meet these two clubs again a little later.)

These firms emulated the Mods and Rockers of the sixties: gangs of aggressive young men out to prove themselves in gang fights, united in a spurious loyalty, either to a particular fashion culture or to a football club. In the case of the latter, the aim and focus were more on fighting than supporting the team. In many cases, the mass battles were arranged by the opponents to take place outside the stadium during the match, though that didn't save those caught in the wrong place at the wrong time and wearing the wrong-coloured scarf from a doing-over. The gang ethos, and the extremes to which the violence could escalate, were explored – some would say celebrated – in the film *Green Street* and follow-ups, which certainly captured the adrenaline rush of combat.

But mostly, hooliganism sparked off in the grounds themselves, when the taunting and jeering escalated into the throwing of missiles, seats and, where possible, punches. In 1974, an FA Cup quarter-final between Newcastle United and Nottingham Forest exploded into a massive pitch invasion with fighting between the two sets of fans. The tie was abandoned. Manchester United's relegation from Division 1 that same season unleashed a wave of terror from the marauding Red Army, taking out their rage on Division 2 clubs up and down the land. Another relegation battle – between Chelsea and Tottenham Hotspur in 1975 – blew up into another pitch battle, while the FA Cup Quarter final in 1978 between Millwall and Ipswich Town started with fighting on the terraces that spread onto the playing area, where it developed into a full-scale riot, spilling onto the streets outside, causing dozens of injuries.

This shocking behaviour did not go unremarked, and police, politicians and the game's administrators came up with various palliative measures like sectioning off areas of grounds for away supporters or erecting metal fences to prevent pitch invasions (which, in conjunction with police incompetence, proved disastrous at Hillsborough). The hard core became more sophisticated, casting off their club favours to infiltrate the away supporters' areas and, when the game began, leaping into action like the Greeks emerging from the wooden horse to massacre the unsuspecting Trojans.

The trouble got worse as the 1980s progressed – and not just in the big cities but up and down the country, though only excessive eruptions of violence were deemed worthy of news coverage. One instance was the FA Cup quarter-final between Luton Town and Millwall in March 1985. And I was there to witness it.

The harsh winter weather of January and February that year meant that a number of FA Cup fixtures were behind schedule as games were cancelled. Luton and Watford were drawn together for the second season running, this time in round five, which gave us the chance of revenge after our local rivals had beaten us in 1984, going on all the way to the final. The fifth-round match was played at Kenilworth Road on Monday, 4th March, and I was one of the 18,000-strong crowd willing Luton to win. It was an epic derby encounter, with no holds barred, but although both sides battered each other and there were chances at both ends, it finished 0-0, with a replay 48 hours later. Luton went down the road to Watford to do it all over again.

I didn't make it, as I was at school when the tickets went on sale – no barcodes on mobile phones in those days! And no television coverage for a match of that status either, so I had to listen to the radio commentary. This is a form of torture because, however good the commentary, you can't see the build-up play, so your anticipation depends on the tone and volume of the commentator's voice. Twice that went into goal mode, in Watford's favour, leaving Luton with a mountain to climb. But with more screeching crescendos, the Hatters came back to gain a heroic draw, which triggered a third replay, which this time came three days later on the Saturday (9th March).

I wasn't missing that, so I bunked off school on the Thursday to secure my ticket. Which meant I was there to see Wayne Turner score the deciding goal in the second replay to take us into the sixth round for the first time since 1973. And our opponents? Millwall, from Division 3 as it was then. The game was scheduled for the following Wednesday (13th March) at Kenilworth Road. The tight timescale made it impossible for the match to be an all-ticket affair, which meant it was turn up and pay on the night. Was that a good idea?

I didn't care. I was going, and all I wanted was to get through an interminable day at school. By the afternoon, I was convinced the hands of the classroom clock had stopped. The bell would never ring. I would be stuck sucking the end of my biro trying to pretend to be interested in ox-bow lakes for the rest of time. But at last the torment was over and I led the stampede to escape.

The first thing that Mum said as I threw myself into the passenger seat was, 'I hope you're not going to the game.' What?! *Of course* I was going to the game. She shook her head. 'There's been lots of trouble already,' she said. 'Rubbish, it's only 4 o'clock,' I didn't reply, realising that I had to tread carefully if I didn't want to be faced with a curfew.

And actually, she was right. Millwall fans had been arriving from lunchtime onwards, set on terrorising the town. Mum put the car radio on and there were reports of hooliganism and running skirmishes with the police. The message was clear: stay at home. But I was going with Dad, as usual, so that was all right, wasn't it? It was the furthest we'd come in the Cup for over ten years, and back then I was three, so I had to go. After much tutting, dark looks at Dad over tea and many warnings to stay safe, we set off for the ground.

My main emotion was intense excitement, but there was trepidation in the mix as well – especially when, as we walked along Maple Road on the approach to the stadium, we met a stream of Luton supporters hurrying the other way, strongly advising us to turn around and head home. But we pressed on regardless.

It may seem surprising but, when we got to the gates, we did as we always did – separate. Dad went to sit in the main stand and I made my way into the

Oak Road terrace where I wouldn't embarrass him by the exuberance of my celebrations. It wasn't difficult to find a good place to stand, though I didn't know at the time that there was so much room because a lot of Luton fans had thought better of it and left. The other thing I didn't know was that the turnstiles at the away end had been stormed.

But I could see the result. All hell was breaking loose as the Millwall mob overflowed from the stands and hundreds of them spilt onto the pitch and set off in a beeline to attack the home fans. I'd never seen anything like it and, partly because I was fifteen, assumed I'd be safe on my usual terrace whatever happened because I was surrounded by my fellow Hatters.

The pitch invaders soon turned into terrace invaders, all keen to come to blows with anyone wearing a Luton scarf. There was a strong plea over the tannoy from the Millwall manager, George Graham, who must have been worried that, unless sanity was restored, his club would simply be expelled from the Cup. He was authoritative enough to get most of the visiting fans back to their terrace, but I could see quite a few infiltrating the main stand and starting punch-ups. As that was where Dad was sitting, I was worried for him.

> " This was not what the Millwall fans had come to see.

The police with their dogs were clearing the pitch by this stage, and, amazingly, the match actually began on time. But 14 minutes later, trouble broke out again, and play was halted for 25 minutes. Not the ideal conditions for an important Cup tie, but maybe all the mindless aggravation got under the Luton lads' skin. Brian Stein scored the first goal – to tumultuous applause – and we looked to have the determination to keep that slender lead through to the end.

This was not what the Millwall fans had come to see. As the game neared the final whistle, the touchlines were thronged with police and would-be pitch invaders trying to break through to disrupt the game's dying moments. The aim was clearly to get the match abandoned so there'd be another chance to win the tie.

It didn't happen. I don't remember much additional time, and when the ref blew the final whistle, the officials and both teams broke Olympic sprint records to reach the safety of the dressing rooms. The Millwall mob regrouped as a fighting force and ransacked the Bobbers Stand, trashing seats for missiles to hurl at the police as they surged towards the home supporters for one last attempt at hand-to-hand combat.

I was stunned as I watched all this unfolding right in front of me. I must have had enough adrenaline pumping through my system to stop me being frightened. But I was shocked at how many fans there were fighting each other just yards away. The noise was unbelievable, with the police dogs barking, policemen bellowing orders – vocally supported by our fans – and then the yelling and swearing of dozens of grown men clawing, kicking and punching each other as though they were on a medieval battlefield.

Thanks to the bravery and discipline of the police, the thin blue line held, and the rabble were eventually overwhelmed and dispersed. At least in the stadium, the action was over. As the home supporters drained out of the terrace, I could see the sharp-edged pound coins the Millwall fans had thrown at us – which emphasised the seriousness of the threat we had come under. Making sure I stayed close to other Hatters, I went out to meet Dad at our usual place to celebrate the fact that we had both survived the match unharmed.

It was only then that I fully realised what a footballing achievement I had witnessed: Luton were now in the FA Cup semi-final! We went home happy with that, but by an unspoken agreement played down the storm of thuggish hostility that had overshadowed a great sporting event.

The Millwall militia carried on in the same vein, smashing cars and shop windows and terrifying local residents on their way back to the station for their trains to London. This was what dominated the front pages the following morning and drew editorial condemnation of the state of things in the national game. Thirty-one people were arrested and appeared in court the next day. Tellingly, many of the culprits claimed to be supporters of Chelsea or West Ham, not Millwall.

The aftermath was not very edifying. An FA inquiry fined Millwall £7,500 for the damage their supporters had caused, but this was withdrawn on appeal. And Luton were ordered to put up fences around the ground, which was also reversed on appeal.

I don't remember what sentences – if any – the courts handed down to those found guilty. But the obvious conclusion to be drawn was that basically a small army of thugs could rampage through a town and come close to sabotaging an important football match with little risk of serious punishment. The fact that the match was shown on BBC *Sportsnight* was shaming, but at least the parlous state of the game was there for all to see.

And 1985 had even more horrors to come.

It was a dark year for the game, with the Bradford City stadium fire of 11th May causing the deaths of 56 spectators, with at least another 250 injured. The ground was filled, as this was the day Bradford received the Third Division championship trophy. The main stand had already been condemned and a replacement was due after the season ended. A cigarette butt fell through a hole in the flooring, igniting a pile of uncleared rubbish. A brisk wind quickly stirred up a tornado of flames, panic seized the crowd stampeding to escape. Many perished at the turnstiles where the gates had been locked at kick-off.

On the same day, another episode in the grim saga saw another fatality when a young boy died as a result of fighting between Birmingham City and Leeds United fans at the St Andrew's stadium. Justice Popplewell, chairman of an investigation into football hooliganism, called the incident more like the Battle of Agincourt than a football match.

Those who thought things couldn't get any worse were appalled three weeks later when, on 29th May, Liverpool fans set about another battle reenactment at the Heysel Stadium in Brussels, which was hosting the European Cup final. The Merseysiders broke through a police cordon to charge Juventus fans. Many fleeing Italian supporters were crushed by a wall that collapsed through the sheer weight of bodies. The whole event was a shambles. Those who went simply to support their team reported complete chaos, with tickets not even asked for and incompetent policing. That the ageing stadium was not fit for purpose is clear, though none of that excuses the disgraceful behaviour of the Liverpool supporters. The night of shame was made even more shocking by the decision that the match should still be played, despite the death toll, which finally reached 39.

There were consequences. All English football clubs were banned from European competitions until 1990, with Liverpool suspended for a further year. This seemed unfair to many fans – and indeed it was the usual story of the many suffering as a result of the behaviour of the few – but Liverpool was by no stretch of the imagination the only club whose supporters created violent mayhem, and the strict sanctions delivered a strong message.

Not that fans took much notice to begin with. In 1986, Leeds supporters ran riot in the temporary home of Bradford City, pushing over and setting fire to a fish and chip van only a year after the deadly fire that had destroyed much of their ground. A year later, thousands of Wolves fans ran amok through the streets of Scarborough to mark their first away match of the Division Four season. The sedate seaside resort had never seen such wanton destruction and unprovoked violence. A year later, Millwall were involved in another battle, this time with Arsenal supporters, resulting in 40 arrests.

Compared with the Falklands War, the miners' strike and the seemingly endless bombing campaigns of the IRA, football hooliganism might seem insignificant, but by mid-decade Mrs Thatcher was exasperated by the harm it was doing to the nation's image. The Heysel Disaster was front page news around the globe, and the government had to be seen to be doing something to turn the hooligan tidal wave. A war cabinet to achieve this was set up, and the Popplewell Committee given the brief to uncover the roots of the problem. At the same time, it was recognised that the grounds were often run-down and unsafe, while the proximity of the standing crowds to the pitch was obviously a danger. Pitch invasions were commonplace, putting both officials and players at risk. But the wire fences erected to keep crowds at bay, though installed as a safety measure, also had the potential to be anything but.

As the final act of this dismal decade, there was Hillsborough, with nearly twice the number of fatalities than at Bradford City. The first assumption for many – especially given that Liverpool were again involved in a major incident – was it was just another example of delinquent behaviour. Barristers acting for the police claimed that their actions – or inactions – had been in response to the threat of hooliganism, while the press, led by *The Sun*, assumed the Scousers had brought the tragedy on their own heads. The UEFA President, Jacques Georges, simply described the Liverpool fans as 'beasts'.

Having seen the dark side of English football close up and watched the far worse events of Hillsborough unfold on live television, I could only feel sick at the state of things. A tiny but virulent minority were sabotaging the sport. I felt strong empathy with that majority of ordinary football fans traipsing loyally, and at no little expense, up and down the country to support their teams. I could only hope that Hillsborough would draw a line under a tragic decade and that the nineties would be a whole lot better.

CHAPTER CHALLENGES ANSWERS

1. *Wayne Rooney – aged 17 years and 317 days v FYR Macedonia in September 2003.*

2. *Bobby Moore – aged 22 years and 47 days v Czechoslovakia in May 1963.*

CHAPTER 4

Maturity

Me, Gazza and Marriage

1990 was World Cup year. The England team qualified for the finals in Italy and, with a strong team captained by Bryan Robson and including Peter Shilton, Paul Gascoigne, Gary Lineker, Chris Waddle and Stuart Pearce, seemed to have a good chance of going far. Unfortunately, with the Heysel catastrophe still very much a living memory and the general association of England fans with violence and mayhem, the team were forced to play all their Group matches on the island of Sardinia. Despite a heavy police presence, there were still disturbances, and it's probably a fair bet that the home nation hoped England never made it to the mainland.

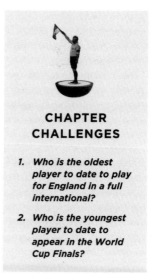

CHAPTER CHALLENGES

1. **Who is the oldest player to date to play for England in a full international?**

2. **Who is the youngest player to date to appear in the World Cup Finals?**

They did though, and after a bruising quarter-final with Cameroon, the surprise package of the tournament, they met West Germany in the semi-final. Was I there? I wasn't. I didn't even watch the match. Instead, I was working in the Food Service team at Camp Sea Gull, North Carolina. No soccer training, but lots of burger flipping. I was no longer the innocent abroad and was probably less interested in organised sport than in the fun I was having with my friends at the camp. I certainly had a different mindset from the young boy who opted to stay on at school to watch every England World Cup match rather than go on the family holiday to France in 1982.

Although the US had made it to the finals, that didn't make Americans interested in the competition. Soccer was never going to reach the heights of the Super Bowl. The matches were all played at the wrong time, so television coverage was virtually non-existent. We were years off the 24/7 news coverage of the internet. I kept in touch with home of course, though my phone calls always coincided with England match days.

When we made it through to the semi-final against West Germany, I was on tenterhooks. All I could do was arrange a call from Mum, who had the joyless task of telling me the awful news: England had lost on penalties, Stuart Pearce and Chris Waddle proving the unlucky ones who failed to score. I was gutted to have missed a rollercoaster of a match, which for long periods England looked like winning. Instead, I had to glean the bare bones of the game, culminating in the stark report of penalties missed and the chance of glory squandered. Thanks, Mum! (Don't shoot the messenger.)

And it wasn't as though I had anyone to sympathise with me. The Americans didn't care, as they had never been serious competitors. But there were some football fans from across the Pond. Unfortunately, they were Irish and delighted in giving me ceaseless stick. I finally got to see the highlights two months later when I was home again. I have to say, I didn't watch with much enthusiasm.

But life in the nineties was good. Once I got my BTEC, I was qualified to enter the leisure industry. My first full time job was as duty manager at Batchwood Golf and Tennis Centre, St Albans, which suited me well – and left plenty of time to continue officiating in the Chiltern Youth League and other matches as they cropped up. And of course, I remained a keen football supporter.

The most memorable match for me of the 1991/92 season was the European Cup final at Wembley. That England got to host Europe's most important game was a sign that we had been accepted back into the fold. Needless to say though, neither of the two clubs fighting for the highest honours was English. Barcelona beat Sampdoria 1-0 in a display of disciplined and highly skilled football. The Italian and Spanish fans mingled happily in the early summer sunshine, coming together at the stadium to create a wonderfully exciting but completely unthreatening atmosphere in the evening. Fervent singing, unfurled banners, waving flags and dazzling flares showed the host nation how these things should be done, and the whole day as a total joy.

But the unacceptable side of English football persisted: grudging, mean, aggressive, violently partisan and always seemingly on the brink of actual violence. I had decided to give the adult game another go, readily accepted into the fold by the North Home Counties League. But that didn't last even a month. I just couldn't put up with the abuse, criticism and constant hostility.

And that dark undercurrent still accompanied the professional game now that we were welcomed back to Europe. Perhaps 'welcomed' is the wrong word. The various European police forces tasked with keeping English fans in check did not come across as particularly friendly. Not surprising, given how much time they spent dealing with fans drinking themselves into a state of aggressive intoxication.

In June 1992, I travelled to Sweden to watch England play in Euro '92. It was my first England away trip. I was with a group of friends, and we kept out of the trouble spots, but the atmosphere was like the prelude to a storm. Trouble was just waiting to break out. And when it did, mounted police appeared in numbers and were soon charging the inebriated English fans who were smashing up café tables and hurling chairs in the main square in Malmo.

Earlier in the evening, as I was buying a lemonade, I'd got talking to a Swedish girl and, yes, she was stunningly beautiful. She was also generous – and quick-witted, whisking me away from the melee on the back of her bicycle. What happens on tour stays on tour, but my night was a great improvement on what my friends imagined for me. A comfy bed and a cooked breakfast in the morning beats sleeping bags in a tent. When I returned to the campsite, there was considerable interest in how I'd spent the intervening hours.

> " Mounted police were soon charging the inebriated English fans.

'Hi, Gav! What happened to you? Did you get arrested? How was your night in the cells?'

Giving up on trying to repress a broad grin, I told them what had actually happened.

The England team's visit to Sweden was less rewarding than mine, and after the disappointing 0-0 draw against Denmark, there was another goalless draw against France before a 1-2 defeat by Sweden saw us exiting the competition at the Group stage. Even with both Gary Lineker and Alan Shearer in the squad, the team simply didn't score enough goals. Many blamed the manager, Graham Taylor, who was pilloried by *The Sun*, with its 'Turnip Head' image, just underlining that the job of England manager is probably the worst in world football.

At my more modest level, I had decided to give playing another go after I'd given up on adult refereeing. I registered with Wheathampsted FC in the Review Sunday League. We got to the Junior Cup final and came a close second in a 2-3 defeat. Worse than a runner's-up medal was a renewal of my medical problem, and a month after my adventures in Malmo, I went in for my third operation on that troublesome left knee to have ligament and cartilage damage attended to.

The following season, I went even further afield, watching England play in Turkey, Poland and Norway. In March 1993, I went on a day trip to Izmir to watch England beat Turkey 2-0. There were only two flights home after the match, and as the players wanted to get back that night, they had to mix with the fans in the departure lounge. Paul Gascoigne was in his element, just one of the lads, while basking in the adoration he always received from English supporters. It turned into Gazza's party.

There was, predictably enough, a crush at the bar, but it didn't take Gazza long to join the bar staff and speed up the delivery of litres and litres of lager. He saw me in the throng and shouted an offer of a drink, but in a moment of maturity I declined. My car was parked at Gatwick, and I had to drive it home. On our return, the police were out in force, and every driver leaving the car park at Gatwick was stopped and breathalysed. A green light for me, but lots of the others were caught out.

> " Paul Gascoigne was in his element, just one of the lads.

A couple of months later, I was on a supporters' bus to Katowice to see England draw 1-1 with Poland. Anticipating the usual aggression from England fans, the locals attempted to get their retaliation in early, to borrow a well-known phrase from Leeds legend, Billy Bremner. They assaulted the taxis taking us to the stadium, trying to smash windscreens with a hail of stones. The match went ahead without misbehaviour by the English fans. However, understandably, the taxi drivers refused to risk taking us back to the hotel after the match, so the England supporters formed up together, all domestic rivalries forgotten in the common cause, and led by some very hard men from an assortment of clubs, marched the couple of miles back into town.

At some point the road went through thick woods, and suddenly dozens of Poles appeared intent on barring our way. Our leaders simply marched on, and it was the would-be assailants who thought better of it and slunk back into the forest. The local police, having cottoned on to the likelihood of trouble, turned up after the showdown and officiously escorted us the rest of the way back to the hotel.

The footballing magical mystery tour continued through Germany, Denmark and Sweden to Oslo, where we saw England lose 0-2 to Norway. The evening before the game, a hard core of England fans went on the rampage, drawing a robust response from the police. This running battle got all the media coverage. Meanwhile, half a mile away, my mates and I were enjoying a sociable evening with a group of friendly locals in a bar playing pool, eating pizza and talking football. Exactly as it should have been. It was just a pity England's performance was so poor.

I was now playing for Bedford Arms in the Leighton and District League – this despite, or rather because of, my third knee operation. In January 1993, I was playing in a Sunday morning match when two players jumped for the same ball and, with the sound of a couple of coconuts, banged together, fell apart and lay groaning on the turf. It turned out I had the best first aid qualifications, so I put my training to good use, having told someone to ring 999. One of the players had actually fractured his skull, so knowing what to do before the real medics arrived was a useful contribution, for which I was later given the 'Clubman' award.

My appetite for travel was unabated, and in October 1993, I went to Rotterdam to see England play Holland. There was tight security throughout the day, with a heavy escort to and from the ground. We were made to feel like prisoners let out for a day's hard labour. And watching England going down 2-0 was pretty severe punishment, especially as the defeat almost certainly guaranteed our exclusion from the World Cup finals – and the end of Taylor's career as England manager. A passionate man, he left himself open to mockery when his impulsive reaction to misfortune came out in a hilarious jumble – 'Do I not like that?!' – which gave the press yet another stick to beat him with.

England had a mathematical chance to go through if they could defeat San Marino in Bologna by 7 goals and if the Dutch obligingly lost to Poland. It was a long shot, but I was up for another lengthy pilgrimage to the shrine of far-fetched optimism. But we missed the coach in London, and even though we leapt onto a train to Dover, we failed to catch the coach up before it got on the ferry. At least we tried.

After the long and futile slog to and from the south coast, I was duly installed in front of the television the following night for what promised to be a memorable if nerve-wracking evening. Graham Taylor told his men that if they brought it off, their names would be inscribed in the memories of England supporters for ever. As it turned out, the game did immortalise one player for a moment of impulsive genius – but he wasn't

  ❝❝ All domestic rivalries forgotten in the common cause.

playing for England. We didn't have to wait very long to witness it.

The two teams came out: England's finest towering over their amateur opponents. The anthems were played. The handshakes and flags were exchanged, and the coin flipped. San Marino were to kick off and the commentators started to explain that England had to win by 7 goals – breaking off after 8 seconds as the home team scored the first goal of the match. 8.33 seconds to be precise, which was and is likely to remain the fastest goal in World Cup history.

It was scored by Davide Gualtieri, an electrician by trade, and he certainly injected a spark into the proceedings when he streaked onto a feeble back pass from Stuart Pearce and left David Seaman for dead as he slotted the ball home to give the visitors the shock of their lives.

Normal service was resumed, and England dutifully went about accumulating 7 goals, but that still left them one short of the requirement. Fortunately for all concerned, that became irrelevant with Holland's defeat of Poland, which closed the door on Taylor's sub-par team. It was the first time in 16 years that England had failed to qualify for the World Cup finals, and six days later Graham Taylor resigned, much to the delight of the red-tops.

Like everyone else, I watched Gualtieri's lightning strike in disbelief – and probably thought I'd done well not to have made the long trip to see England made to look foolish. For make no mistake, Gualtieri's goal is the only thing the match will be remembered for.

To counter my disappointment as an England fan, Luton had a great FA Cup run, and I was a faithful supporter. I certainly showed stickability. When in January 1994 my Vauxhall Cavalier broke down en route to Newcastle, the AA came to the rescue and towed me and my pal Paul into Nottingham, where we quickly hired another car and carried on, determined not to miss the game. Fuelled by the Hatters' 1-1 away draw, I drove all the way home in the hire car, keeping it till Monday morning when I got up very early to drive it back to hire company by 9.00, before getting the train home from Nottingham in time to be only marginally late for work. I never saw the Cavalier again. I just bought a replacement from Dad's forecourt and left him to sort out the Vauxhall. He didn't seem to mind.

Luton kept going in the Cup, reaching the semi-final, where they met Chelsea. Wembley was the Neutral Venue and was absolutely packed with hordes of Hatters hoping they could keep going while knowing this was always going to be a tough one. Chelsea were in the recently created Premier League but weren't doing any better than their mid-table performances in previous years, despite the arrival of new player-manager, Glenn Hoddle. We were in what was now Division 1, so there was a big gulf in class. They pulled out all the stops against us and sailed comfortably into the final, winning

2-0. (The final, though, was a disaster for them: 0-0 at half time dissolved into a crushing defeat as Manchester United scored four unanswered goals.)

I was playing for Red Lion Leighton in the Leighton and District League and enjoying my run-arounds on Sunday morning. Life was all right and I was perfectly happy; but I wasn't happy that everything was perfect. It was time to move on in life and geographically. In the summer, I moved south to become Duty Manager at Salisbury Leisure Centre.

Life in Wiltshire wasn't very different from life in Bedfordshire. I did the same sort of work and found a football team to join. But the change I felt I was ready for came in 1995. I got a bang on the head when I clashed with another player's elbow on a Tuesday evening in May. It was a nasty one and maybe it was the wake-up call I needed. That summer, I got married and, as part of the general readjustment, finally decided that I wasn't good enough to continue playing football. My ambitions to play professionally had seeped away, and I had got tired of being a sub – or being subbed mid-game at the whim of a coach whom I didn't particularly respect. I realised that I wanted to be involved in all of the game. And the only way that was going to happen was if I revived my refereeing career.

I contacted Wiltshire FA and, after an orientation interview in October 1995, was soon registered as a Class 3 referee with them. At 25 rather than 15, I was more mature, more experienced and had far better prospects. I now had an understanding of the pathway available to me and a strong determination to get as far down that path as I could.

CHAPTER CHALLENGES ANSWERS

1. *Stanley Matthews – aged 42 years and 104 days v Denmark in May 1957.*

2. *Norman Whiteside – aged 17 years and 41 days for Northern Ireland v Yugoslavia in June 1982 (Spain '82).*

PART 2

SIDELINE OR

FRONTLINE?

CHAPTER 5
_____

Earning My Stripes

Rungs on the Ladder

I was only in Wiltshire for a couple of years, but those years were pivotal. In my first season, I refereed 24 matches in the Salisbury and District League and also ran the line in five Wiltshire County League games. From 1996 onwards, linesmen were referred to as assistant referees, or ARs for short. To extend my skillset and my involvement with the game, I took the FA coaching course and started coaching youngsters at the Leisure Centre.

CHAPTER CHALLENGES

Although I enjoyed every aspect of my work there, I didn't get on well with the manager, who once cautioned me for leaving work three minutes early to travel to an evening game I was refereeing. I was issued with a formal written warning. Our relationship, unsurprisingly, plummeted.

But no petty killjoy could cast a shadow over the glorious festival of football that summer of 1996. We were hosting the European Championship and I saw every England game. The sun seemed to shine throughout June, and particularly on the England team under the charismatic management of Terry Venables. After a 1-1 draw against Switzerland, England went up through the gears, defeating Scotland – 'that goal' – and then beating the much-fancied

1. *A player commits a foul that is worthy of a caution. Before you have a chance to issue the card, the opposing team takes a quick free kick. What do you do?*

2. *A player on the bench throws a water bottle towards an opponent who is on the field of play while the ball is in play. What do you do?*

Dutch 4-1. The quarter-final against Spain was a dogged defensive exercise which went all the way to penalties. England survived the nail-biting ordeal (4-2) to go through the even tougher challenge of Germany in the semi-final.

Germany were probably favourites to repeat their success of the 1990

47

World Cup semi-final. Although Alan Shearer scored the opening goal after three minutes, the Germans equalised almost immediately, and a fierce battle of attrition ensued. The score was still 1-1 after 90 minutes, pushing the contest into extra time. Paul Gascoigne had the chance to clinch a place in the final when Shearer, put through by Sheringham, sent a pass into the box, only for it to elude Gazza's outstretched boot with the goal gaping. After the drama of a disallowed goal at the other end, the two teams had to re-enact the penalty shoot-out of six years before.

While the nation's fans gnawed their fingernails, covered their eyes, took the dog for a walk, vacuumed the car, hid in the wardrobe or whimpered behind the sofa, the first five players on each side slotted home. Gareth Southgate, the young defender, stepped up to take England's sixth and failed to find the net. Andreas Möller made no mistake, and Germany were through to another final, which, needless to say, they won, beating the Czech Republic 2-1 with a golden goal in extra time.

> Germany were through to another final.

I was at Wembley for the final, having hoped when I booked the ticket that I would be watching England lifting a trophy to match the triumph of 1966. The team had been splendid – both dazzling in attack – Gazza's brilliant goal against the Scots – but also robust and reliable in defence. All England fans were convinced that if we'd got to the final, we'd have had the beating of the Czechs. But we can never know. For all the disappointment, it had been a wonderful tournament, and I was there every step of the way (which beat waiting for a phone call from my Mum in the States as I had been for the last penalty shoot-out against the Germans).

Glad though I was to have arranged my allocation of leave so that I could attend all six matches, I was still not happy at work. I gave notice and got a new job in Dunstable that autumn. Uprooting the family was not on the cards, so I did a weekly commute over the winter before settling my wife and young daughter in Luton in February 1997.

It might look as though I had retreated to my comfort zone with my tail between my legs, but a lot happened in those two years in Wiltshire, and I returned home a husband, a father and someone dedicated to making a career as a football official. I re-registered with Bedfordshire and was soon refereeing in the North Home Counties League and running the line in the Luton and South Beds League.

I was getting more appointments than ever before – 74 in 1997/98, which was my first full season back. That was a record for me – as was the number of matches I watched: 0. This reflected my new status as a dad, and of course I didn't begrudge the limits on the time I could give the game. As a treat at the end of the season, I went to Lens to watch the World Cup match between England and Columbia, which we won 2-0.

During the close season, I was promoted from Class 3 to Class 2, which meant I officiated at a slightly higher level. As I edged up the pecking order, I found myself officiating before larger crowds, which exposed me to the increased aggression of the more fanatical fans. In November 1998, I found myself at Kenilworth Road as an assistant referee. It was the Southern Junior Floodlit Cup, and it was a strange but invigorating experience to walk down the tunnel and onto the pitch I knew so well as an official rather than a spectator. Luton Town beat Northampton Town 3-1.

The same month, I also ran the line in a match between two rival Luton clubs in a Carlsberg Club match. It was a Sunday afternoon, and the assumption was that it would be played in a friendly spirit, so there was no security. There was a big crowd and as the game went to the wire, the supporters became first raucous and then positively unpleasant. As linesman, you have your back to your critics, and whatever the jeers about your eyesight (or indeed about your pedigree), you just have to stay focused on getting your decisions right.

The final score was 3-4, which probably reflected the number of pints consumed by a large percentage of those who attended. The defeated side's fans were strangers to the concept of losing graciously and, with no security to protect us, the match officials kissed goodbye to their dignity and legged it to the changing rooms on the other side of the park, pursued by a howling mob armed with pint glasses. Happily, few of them could call on the level of fitness required of us, so all was well.

The fitness test was a serious undertaking and had to be undergone every year. I took mine at Stockwood Park Athletic Track and had to go into training for the Cooper Test, which required covering a minimum of 2,600 metres in 12 minutes. You were always under scrutiny, and in addition to being super-fit,

> " The match officials kissed goodbye to their dignity.

you had to keep up to date with any Law changes that were introduced. I wanted to raise my game and, as the Millennium approached, pushed for and got my promotion, so I entered the new century as a Class 1 referee.

This promotion brought invitations to officiate in more important matches. My first match as an AR in the Southern League seemed a massive event. The players were actually being paid to play and performances – my own included – were judged at a higher level. Instead of one man shouting on the touchline, there were managers and coaches in the technical area. This was professional football, albeit it at entry level.

We were expected to turn up wearing a collar and tie and faced a strict assessment on all facets of our performance from the match assessor. It was a very hot day, which made it more demanding. I tried to quell my nerves and remind myself that I had done enough to earn my involvement at this level. The game was a 2-2 draw between Raunds Town and Dartford. Once the whistle blew, it was simply another game, with me making sure I was in the right place to make the right decisions. Which I clearly did because my assessor was happy with me.

There were other firsts that autumn of 1999 – linesman in the FA Vase, linesman in the FA Premier Academy (Spurs beat Crystal Palace 3-2), and then linesman in the FA Cup for the first time, a third-round qualifying tie between Enfield and Billericay Town. This was played just down the road at St Albans City FC's ground and ended in a 2-0 win for Enfield. I also ran the line in the FA County Youth Cup – a close game in which Northamptonshire beat Cornwall 4-3. I enjoyed this, as there were potential stars of the future involved, though it has to be said they played at such a high tempo I was kept busy keeping up.

That challenge was not made any easier by a recurrence of problems with my left knee. November 1999 had seen me trollied into theatre for my fourth operation: tibial osteotomy, resulting in my left leg disappearing into a plaster sarcophagus for two months. This hampered my celebrations of both Christmas and the Millennium. But once the plaster was off, I made a quick recovery, got back into training and was able to return to football for the last six weeks of the season.

After the summer break in August 2000, I was invited to run the line in a pre-season friendly between Bedford Town and Luton – my own team. That was only permissible in a friendly – and yes, the powers-that-be do delve into your affiliations, for obvious reasons when you think about it. It was a bit weird seeing the players and managers close up and hearing the crowd without being part of it – as though I'd somehow got through the wrong gate and would soon be exposed as an interloper. But I really was a *bona fide* assistant referee, with the kit and the flag and my heart beating in anticipation of the match ahead.

Once the whistle blows and the game starts, you lose all sight of who's playing. It's just two teams, blue v white, and your job is to focus on being the best linesman you can be. You can't let anything distract you – not the crowd, not the players. Even when someone scores a brilliant goal, you have to stay focused. All you have to be sure of is that the goal-scorer was on side and that the ball crossed the line. In this instance, I enjoyed the deferred gratification of the Hatters winning 4-3. It was a good game, but the more important thing was that I had a good game. Progress up the ladder meant getting it right. All the time.

And by the end of the season, I had got it right enough times to be invited to attend an interview in London for promotion to the referees list for the Southern League. I passed and got a letter of confirmation that I was on the referees list for the following season.

It may seem confusing that I divided my time between refereeing and running the line, but as the title 'assistant referee' indicates, every AR is a qualified referee. They are obviously two very different roles, but ARs have to know all aspects of the game just as well as referees. After all, one of them will have to replace a referee who gets incapacitated during a match. In professional football, there are at least four officials – one referee, two running the line and a fourth to deal with substitutions, over-excited managers, and anything else that has a potential impact on the game. All four work as a team, with the referee for the day the team leader. Although my stand-out matches in 2000/01 had been as a linesman, I was judged not only by my ability to call an offside accurately, but also to run a whole game with a whistle attached to my wrist.

My first experience as referee in the Southern League was in August 2001, Rothwell Town v Dorchester Town. I am always on time – for everything – but particularly for football matches. On this occasion, I was at the ground

The first tackle seemed like a car crash.

two hours before I needed to be. Which meant I had too much time pacing around getting ever more nervous. When I came to give my pre-match talk to the rest of my team, I decided to sit down in an attempt to look relaxed. I don't know if it worked, but it stopped me nervously stepping from one foot to the other. It was a relief to lead the way onto the pitch, supervise the toss and finally blow the whistle to start the action.

This was serious, big boys' stuff. The first tackle seemed like a car crash. I felt like a policeman on a bicycle trying to control the traffic on a motorway. But after a few calls for fouls which didn't cause the players to tear me limb from limb, my confidence rose. I'd been doing this for years – albeit at a lower level. I knew the Laws, and, as a player myself, I could read the game. I could interpret the antics of the players – the perfectly timed dive, the deliberately late challenge. A warning look ('I'm onto you, son'), a raised finger ('last warning before a card'); and of course the players' respect grew too as they realised I knew what I was doing.

So when I reached for my red card with ten minutes to go – on the advice of my assistant (teamwork!) – there were no aggressive protestations of innocence, no crowding around to try to get me to reverse my decision. The culprit obviously wasn't pleased, but he went quietly, and the game resumed. When I blew the final whistle ten minutes later, I felt more than relief. As the players shook my hand, clapped me on the back, even muttered, 'Well done, ref', I felt epic.

Another big moment followed in the same month, this time in the Football Conference, Farnborough Town v Barnet, with a crowd of 2,000 on the Bank Holiday Monday. Both managers, Graham Westley and John Still, had strong personalities, i.e. they were determined to get what they wanted and bend others to their will. Barnet had just been relegated from the Football League and were set on going straight back up again, with John Still as manager. I could see it was going to be a pretty intense game.

The intensity level went up a notch or three with an early sending off, and I struggled to concentrate as I was bombarded not just with the usual pleasantries from the crowd but with what amounted to a running commentary (mainly critical) from the technical area. As the senior AR, it was my prerogative to operate on that side of the ground. It often didn't feel like much of a privilege.

For all their endeavours, Barnet failed in their pursuit of three points, Farnborough winning 2-1. Handshakes from the managers differed radically – a brief clench and no eye-contact from the loser, a warm, full grasp and a warm smile with twinkling eyes from the winner. Not surprising really when the stakes are that high. I was just pleased to get back in our little team changing room and start relaxing, reliving the highlights of the game and then thinking about what I was going to do with the rest of my Bank Holiday.

September 2001 is not remembered for anything that happened on a football pitch. 9/11 saw me at Histon FC, where I was down to referee their Southern League match against Fisher Athletic. It was an evening game and I drove to it from work, having heard the news of the assault on the Twin Towers while I was still in the office. On arrival at the ground, my colleagues and I went up to the boardroom to catch up on the news, and it was there I saw the actual footage. It was clear that the world had changed radically in barely an hour. I'm sure if the attack had been on London, all games would have been called off. But although no one felt like playing, the decision was taken that matches were to go ahead. I think we all – players and officials – went through it on autopilot, and I drove home thinking more about what I'd seen on the screen than about the game I'd just refereed. You didn't need to be psychic to know that we were heading into a totally new phase of history.

On the day-to-day level, there wasn't much anyone could do but carry on as normal. It was on the news; plans for retaliation were discussed; Tony Blair seemed to be best friends with George W. Bush. But everybody still had to get up in the morning, get the kids to school, go to work as they always had done. And in my case, that meant climbing into the car on a Saturday afternoon and driving to my next match.

I've said that I am always on time. And I am. Except one Saturday that October, I was 15 minutes late arriving at Grantham. I wasn't late late, and the game started on time, but as per protocol, I reported myself to the League, giving my excuse: an accident on the A1M. Dennis Strudwick, the League secretary, wrote back, pointing out that my being late was still my fault, as I should have allowed enough time for all eventualities. *All*? What if I had been involved in the crash? What if terrorists had blown up a bridge over the motorway? You'd have to get to the ground the night before and sleep in your car if you absolutely had to guarantee you'd be there on time for the match. I'm kidding, of course; but those were febrile days. I kept that letter for many years as a reminder. To this day, that was the only match I've been late for.

In November 2001, I was fourth official in an FA Cup first-round tie between Bedford Town and Peterborough United, along with Phil Joslin, referee, and assistant referees Ray Lee and Darren Cann. So what? Well, it was another first for me, as that was the first televised match I'd officiated in. Of greater note, Darren Cann went on to be linesman in the World Cup final in 2010, which just shows that everybody has to work their way up from the lower levels to reach the absolute pinnacle.

I doubt whether Darren was thinking of World Cup fame as he ran the line that afternoon, and although super keen, I don't suppose I could have outlined my career ambitions at that stage beyond wanting to be involved in the highest level possible. With every step up, the quality of the football increased and the bar for the officials was raised. There was never any room for complacency as you were assessed every match, and you knew that blotting your copybook could result in a brake on future progress. That's one of the reasons why the abuse from fans is so misplaced: every man or woman who dons the black shirt and black shorts and enters the arena with whistle or flag has sweated blood to get there, and although we're all human, thus prone to error, no one regrets mistakes more than we do.

The early noughties saw me making steady progress. I won't bore you with the intricacies of lower-league officialdom, but rest assured there were a lot of hoops to jump through, and I was kept up to standard with regular fitness tests, tests of my knowledge and, of course, unceasing assessment of my performances, whether I was blowing the whistle or waving my flag. Referee classifications were also adjusted – as an existing Class 1, I was now a new Level 3!

A big step up was being given my first opportunity to run the line in the FA Cup first round proper, after so many appearances in the FA Youth Cup and Premier Reserve League. The fact that the two sides, Stevenage Borough and Hastings, were both non-League teams didn't matter. To be appointed to a first-round match showed that your performances were good enough. There were perks as well: they gave you a free kit for the game and paid you FA fees, which were appreciably more than Contributory Leagues fees. This season, 2002/03, I officiated in 69 matches in all.

> How do you break *both* elbows? Simple.

I would probably have matched that the following year but for a bizarre accident that ended my season abruptly after 57 appointments. I managed to break both elbows in an accident. How do you break *both* elbows? Simple. I was showing off on my daughter's scooter and took a purler on a slightly raised slab of pavement, cushioning my impact with my arms. Not to be recommended. Apart from the pain, you become completely dependent in terms of life's most basic requirements with both arms incapacitated.

Luckily, I heal quickly, so being able to do up my flies without assistance was soon followed by being able to wave a flag or blow a whistle. My scores as a referee were getting better and better, and at the end of the season, I was in Band B for Clubs and Band A for Assessors. If you get to A/A, you're pretty well certain of being promoted to the Referees List for the Football Conference and the Assistant Referees List for the Football League. It was only a matter of time.

The following season (2004/05) produced two stand-out occasions. The first came as a complete surprise. I hadn't been able to watch many games in recent years, but I found a spare day to go to the Women's FA Cup sixth-round match between Chelsea and Everton. I had just found my seat and was looking at the programme when I was alerted to a bit of a crisis. It wasn't quite a question of 'Is there a doctor in the ground?' But as the fourth official had failed to turn up, there was a case for me finding a handy telephone box and getting changed. It wasn't quite as dramatic as that. The referee was a mate and knew I was attending, so it was easy enough to draft me in. It was a great game – won 2-0 by Everton, and much more fun being involved than watching from the stand.

A couple of months later, in May (after running the line for the Nationwide Conference Play-Off semi-final first leg between Aldershot Town and Carlisle United, which the Shots won 1-0), I was assistant referee for the FA County Youth Cup final between Suffolk and Hampshire played at Ipswich Town. It was an honour to be involved in an FA final, and everything built up nicely, from the original notification to the day itself, with some serious protocols to observe before the game itself.

Once the whistle went, I was simply focused on the game and always being in the right place to make the right calls. Afterwards I was able to enjoy the presentation (receiving a treasured gold medal) and the post-match banquet. I was on the same table as Ray Tinkler but, to my lasting regret, didn't have the courage to ask him about his take on the notorious Leeds-West Brom match in 1971, which he refereed. West Brom scored an 'offside' goal, won the game 2-1, and Leeds lost their chances of winning the Championship as a result.

I was smashing it as a linesman and felt I was ready to step up to the Football League. But it didn't happen. An FA official had a quiet word. He told me that although my marks as a linesman were good enough, I wasn't scoring well enough as a referee to be promoted. In those days, you had to reach the mark as both. Even if you only wanted to run the line, you had to be up to scratch just in case you were called upon to referee a game. I was stuck where I was for yet another season.

The 2005/06 season was not my finest. I had my usual quota of appointments, 35 as referee, 28 as assistant referee and two as the fourth official. But I did not perform at my usual level, largely because my enthusiasm had slumped after my failure to gain promotion. This was my fifth season at the same level as an assistant. I was now 35 years old and colleagues younger than me were getting promoted while I stayed put, seemingly becalmed. It felt unfair. I was still giving up huge amounts of my time for frankly very little financial reward.

Things in the real world weren't going particularly well either. I had a decent job, having worked my way up to Regional Manager and then Trainer for a company called Teaching Personnel, who had a big stake in the education sector. Basically, if your geography teacher rang in sick half an hour before school assembly, you'd ring us and we'd have a supply teacher on their way before break. Sometimes, things weren't quite as simple as that, and I was often sent off on trouble-shooting missions. Which seemed to fit the skillset I'd developed running around in black shorts with my whistle or flag. My people skills were all about calming things down, pouring oil on troubled water, etc., while still emphasising that rules had to be obeyed and discipline maintained.

Both my day job and my weekend job kept me out of the house a lot of the time, and that impacted life on the home front. This book isn't about that, but suffice it to say the breakup of my marriage to Ruth after ten years in January 2006 was not the ideal start to the New Year. Being kept busy with football helped. I didn't have to spend my weekends rattling around in an empty house. But no one who has ever been through a separation after a long relationship will be surprised to hear that it didn't do much for my general approach to life. There were definitely matches where I was on autopilot, making decisions based on players' reactions and a bit of guesswork rather than on my own clinical observations, and that won't have gone unnoticed. When you're in the doldrums, it feels as though you're going to be there forever.

Flying out to Rio to start a new life in Brazil wasn't an option – though I probably would have been welcomed as a football official. I just had to tough it out and keep on keeping on as best I could. Which sometimes wasn't so good. I had a nightmare game as fourth official for a match in September 2006 between Rushden and Diamonds and Burton Albion. The managers and staff all knew each other, and strong personalities like Nigel Clough, Gary Crosby and Ian Bowyer basically dominated the technical area, leaving me powerless. I was down anyway and didn't have the strength to assert myself. It was a miserable experience, but I determined to learn from it and never let it happen again.

In April 2007, I met Jacqueline and our relationship flourished, giving me a new lease of life, which definitely helped my performances as an official in the following season. My reward was a call-up to run the line for a televised Sunday evening game at Torquay United. It was a reward that involved serious amounts of driving, but I was happy to set off at 10am to meet my colleagues and then drive west to Torquay. It was a long way to go for a 0-0 draw, but I proved that I was up for it – whatever 'it' was. Home at 3.30am. Two hours' kip in an armchair. Alarm at 6am and off to work to help recruit more supply teachers, and as far as I can remember, I managed the day without anyone being sent to the wrong school.

In October 2007, I took charge of the highest-level game I was qualified for as a Level 3 referee – an FA Cup fourth-round qualifier between Maidenhead United and Hayes and Yeading. In April the following year, I ran the line for the televised Conference League Cup – or Setanta Shield – final, in which Aldershot Town beat Rushden and Diamonds on penalties after the match had ended 3-3. The following month, I refereed the FA Academy Under-18 final between Aston Villa and Manchester City. It was a huge honour to referee at Villa Park, and the match went well, with no controversial flashpoints (Villa won 2-0). Afterwards, they gave me an FA Premier League medal.

A really enjoyable season, which had seen me return to my previous best, ended with a letter inviting me to join the National List of Assistant Referees for the following season. This was it. I had at last reached the Football League, a whole new level. Now the hard work really started.

CHAPTER CHALLENGES ANSWERS

1. *Allow the kick to be taken and issue a yellow card for unsporting behaviour at the next stoppage in play.*

2. *Stop play, award a direct free kick to be taken from the place where the bottle interfered with play or struck the opponent or struck the ball.*

CHAPTER 6

Match Day

'Arsène Wenger's having a party/Bring your vodka and your Charlie'

I started the 2008/09 season as a National List assistant referee, but there was a lot to do before the season actually began. There was the fitness assessment, for starters. This took place at Warwick University and here's what it entailed:

6x40m sprints – each under 6.0 seconds, with 90 seconds recovery between each sprint

150m run in under 30 seconds, 40 seconds rest and walk 50m, repeat x 20 (10 laps in total)

BMI measurement

Blood pressure measurement

In June, I attended the PGMOL (Professional Game Match Officials Ltd) conference, listened to a number of instructive and inspirational talks, and was issued with my kit (socks, shorts and shirts x8 – long and short sleeved in four colours) and a very smart kit bag. There was a Polar heart rate monitor thrown in, though experience suggested extreme cold was not something I'd have to worry about very often. We were also given a summer fitness training programme, and then in no time at all I was back at Warwick University doing the pre-season fitness test in mid-July.

The whole football world was gearing up for the new season. Pre-season matches – or mismatches as some seemed – were set up to get teams

CHAPTER CHALLENGES

1. *A player scores a goal then immediately celebrates by removing their shirt. Before you have the chance to caution them, you notice your assistant has ruled the goal offside. What do you do?*

2. *An attacker commits an offence 6m from the defending team's goal. A direct free kick is taken. Where should the attackers be positioned when the kick is taken?*

working together, absorbing summer signings, working on new ideas. I was picked as assistant referee for a match just down the road at Barnet. Who were they playing? Only Arsenal. I spent most of the morning checking that's what the letter really said.

It was a boiling hot day and the Barnet ground was packed with over 5,000 fans. I wore my Football League kit for the first time, feeling like a new boy in his ticklingly new uniform on his first day at school. And who should knock on the match officials' door to deliver his team sheet? Only Arsène Wenger. *Arsène Wenger!* Arguably the most inventive and far-sighted manager of the modern era, who had done so much to change the culture of English football. It's probably a good job he didn't give the team sheet to me, as I'd probably have asked for his autograph. He gave the four of us a tight smile and a nod – which I interpreted as a reminder that his hawk's eye wouldn't miss the slightest blunder – and then we were left just staring at a string of stars whose stickers were traded in primary school playgrounds up and down the country: Manuel Almunia, Bacary Sagna, Gaël Clichy, Theo Walcott, Nicklas Bendtner, Aaron Ramsey – each one of them an international.

And it wasn't long before they were all trotting out onto the pitch and I was pinching myself to check that, yes, I was just about to run the line for 90 minutes of a match they were playing in. The locals were pretty impressed as well, while a lot of Arsenal fans had made it from London for a bit of a day out. Happily, they were better behaved than their Millwall counterparts of 20 years before, though I couldn't help noticing their favourite song, repeated over and over again, featured the line: 'Arsène Wenger's having a party/Bring your vodka and your Charlie', which probably wasn't a reference to Charlie George, whose legendary goal at Wembley won the Gunners the League and FA Cup double in 1971.

No legendary 20-yard strikes at Barnet on that afternoon, and it was clear the visitors were using it more as a training session than a proper match. After all, no one wants to pick up a serious injury in a pre-season friendly against lower-league cannon fodder (though Barnet were good enough to keep the score to a creditable 2-1).

It was a nice warm-up for me as well. No great pressure, no angry gesticulating players or coaches, just an enjoyable celebration of the beautiful game. But things were about to change. In August, I had my first game as an assistant referee in the Football League. It was a League One match between Brighton and Hove Albion and Bristol Rovers. I was super on time for this one – the drive to Brighton in balmy sunny weather was wasted on me, as I was concentrating more on the test ahead than the harvest-ripe fields around me. I found a 'Good Luck' card from a colleague, Keith Hill, when I got to the Withdean Stadium, so everyone knew that this was my first Football League game.

But not my first game ever, I had to remind myself as the nerves jangled and the hands on my watch seemed to go backwards. It was another football match after the hundreds I'd officiated in. A month ago, I'd run the line in a match Arsenal were playing in. It would be fine. But I was desperate for things to go well. I had waited so long for this opportunity to officiate in the highest tier. All I wanted was to be out on the touchline and to get a few calls under my belt.

When I did get out there, my first signal came after 15 minutes. I flagged for an offside, only for the referee (Trevor Kettle) to overrule me, waving play on. It was a terrible start, and for the next few minutes I ran up and down like a zombie, my confidence shattered. I just wanted play to be at the other end of the pitch and for me not to have to make another decision for a good long time. But I had to keep engaged, however I was feeling, and gradually things seemed better. The match, while hard-fought, was uncontroversial. I functioned perfectly competently, keeping pace with the players, and generally producing the anonymous robotic performance expected from the AR.

> 66 I had waited so long for this opportunity.

The final whistle came and I had officiated in a Football League match. No one could take that away from me. And no one would ever remember I'd had an offside call overruled. Even Trevor acknowledged it was close. He just thought I'd possibly been a bit hyper in my first judgment. (No VAR to determine who was right in those days!) No match-winning goal had resulted (it was a pretty tame 1-1 draw), so no harm done.

I drove home smiling inanely and treated myself to a celebratory take-away curry, as Jacqueline was out for the evening. I wanted to share my excitement but realised that even my nearest and dearest might not totally buy into the thrill I felt at having run up and down a white line for 90 minutes without making a complete fool of myself.

Anyway, my next game was an international.

When I got the notification, I seriously thought it was a joke. I'd only been on the National List a month and they were giving me an England match? Pull the other one! But no, it was for real. I would actually be running the line. Admittedly, it was England U17 v Italy U17, and it was at Northampton Town FC not Wembley, but all the same... I walked out with my fellow officials and stood – in the rain – for the two national anthems, and it really felt like the scenes I'd seen so many times on TV. My turn now!

England won 2-0 but, unfortunately, as we know, success at junior level doesn't necessarily translate into triumph for the senior side. After the match, the Italians came to thank us and brought some little tokens of appreciation – pennants and pin badges – which was a nice touch. The whole day was great, and I was pleased with my own performance: tidy, efficient, error-free. I looked forward to more international games to come. I couldn't have known that this would be my one and only.

My first season on the Football League list was a success. I tried my best in every game and wasn't involved in any controversies. I would undoubtedly have got the odd knife-edge offside call wrong, but as we know in these VAR days, the closest calls are very fine margins indeed. I realised that, as a first-year official, I wouldn't get marked too highly by the match assessors. This wasn't an actual policy, more a perceived culture. And not a surprising one when you think of the jump from the lower leagues. A month after my one international, I was running the line in a match between Swindon and Leeds United in front of a crowd of 13,000 – including 4,000 passionate away supporters. Leeds had a player sent off early, which ratcheted things up a bit more. The Laws hadn't changed, your job hadn't changed; but the environment in which you did that job was a different world to what you were used to. I enjoyed it. It was exciting. But you had to be on your mettle every second of the game.

That autumn, I was fourth official for a Championship game at Watford v Cardiff City. As a Luton supporter that felt very weird. But Watford are a brilliant club to visit, and they looked after match officials really well. It was a good game, ending in a 2-2 draw, so I didn't have to witness a Watford win. The following March, I had my first game as assistant referee in a Championship match – Reading v Charlton Athletic. I slipped away from work at lunchtime to get to the Madejski Stadium in good time. It was a great occasion with a big crowd, and a good referee to match. Anthony Taylor went on to much greater things – the Premier League and the FIFA list – so it was a privilege to take the field with him.

I certainly hadn't given up refereeing myself, and at the end of the season took charge of the Football League Youth Alliance League Cup final between Queens Park Rangers and Grimsby Town at Loftus Road. It was a hot spring evening and two good teams showed high skill levels to produce a close contest, which the visitors won 2-1. At the presentation, I collected a Football League medal to go with my FA medal and Premier League medal. Set complete.

Right at the end of the season, I was fourth official for the Southern League Play-Off final but ended up refereeing the last part of the match when Ron Ganfield pulled up with an injury. It's rare, but coming on as a replacement partway through a game always gives you a huge adrenaline rush. It's a bonus and you enjoy it all the more for its being totally unexpected.

The following season (2009/10) had a memorable start. I was fourth official in the Championship match between Crystal Palace and Plymouth Argyle. Mostly, I'd prefer to be actively officiating, but being on the sideline had the advantage of being able to enjoy the game more. And this was an enjoyable game between two well-matched teams who played out a 1-1 draw in the August sunshine. Everything was proceeding as normal, when suddenly the Crystal Palace manager, Neil Warnock, started berating the AR on our side of the pitch over what he felt was a foul throw-in.

Play had gone on and the assistant referee had continued to keep up with the play, but I could see Warnock was still seething, so I went up and asked him what the matter was. He told me the Plymouth player's foot was on the pitch when he took the throw. And he demonstrated the 'offence' by stamping on the line. I looked at Neil's foot and it was partway on the pitch, but not completely over the line.

> 'As 4th Official, you really are on your own.'

'That's allowed,' I said. 'It's like a no ball in cricket – the foot needs to be all the way over the line to be called.'

Neil stared at me, frowning. And then, to his credit, he gave me a slightly shamefaced grin and said simply: 'I never knew that.'

He learned something, and so did I later in the same match. There was another explosion of outrage in the technical area. This time it was one of the Plymouth coaching staff getting upset at something he thought unfairly disadvantaged his team. He grabbed the chewing gum out of his mouth and flung it wildly behind him so he could express his feelings more fluently. It hit me.

Behaviour like that is punishable with a red card, banishing the offender to the stands. I knew that. But I also knew that he hadn't deliberately aimed it at me. No excuse, any more than driving out into traffic without looking excuses you if you hit another vehicle. But although I could have made an issue of it, reported it to the referee the next time play halted, and had him sent on his way, I held back. It would only have exacerbated things and soured the atmosphere – and doubtless have given me a reputation for being a 'little Hitler', a spiteful official always on the lookout for an opportunity to assert his authority. As fourth official, you really are on your own with 20-plus fanatically committed people around you from both technical areas, so it's sensible to pick your battles carefully. You never want to be seen to be weak, because you'll get the reputation for being an easy touch. Being dominated by Clough and Co. a while back had taught me that lesson. But emotional intelligence is an important thing to develop, and I think that game saw me take a step towards being a more complete and understanding official.

Another match that August was to see me and my colleagues tested to the limit in an explosive match which showed the nation that there was still a massive problem in English football.

CHAPTER CHALLENGES ANSWERS

1. *Caution the player for unsporting behaviour and restart with a defensive free kick for the offside offence.*

2. *Outside the penalty area.*

CHAPTER 7
_____

'Look at all the bizzies'

The Riot of Upton Park, Part 1

I got notification that I would be officiating in the West Ham v Millwall League Cup second-round match eight days in advance. Even as I saw my appointment I thought, 'That could be tasty', little knowing that 25th August 2009 would go down as one of the darkest days in the annals of domestic English football.

All local derbies have an edge to them. London derbies can be particularly bitter, especially the one between West Ham and Millwall. Both clubs came from working men's teams dating back to the early 1900s. West Ham originated in a firm called Thames Ironworks, while Millwall were associated with a canning company which serviced two dockyards on either side of the Thames. Even though their geographical proximity diminished over time, and the two sides were seldom in the same division of the League, the intense rivalry continued unabated into the modern era, exacerbated by both sets of supporters developing 'firms' of aggressive thugs in the seventies and eighties.

Thankfully, we're past the heights of football hooliganism, but old antagonisms are not buried very deep beneath the heavily branded veneer of the modern game. It doesn't take much of a spark to light the fuse. Both sets of

CHAPTER CHALLENGES

1. A penalty kick is taken and the shot hits the post. The goalkeeper is on the ground, having tried to save the shot, and the ball rebounds to the penalty taker, who kicks the ball into the unguarded goal. What do you do?

2. Can an attacking player stand next to a three-person defensive wall at a free kick on the edge of the penalty area?

fans inherited generations of antagonism, and so, a Cup match offering the opportunity to take the Premier League West Ham down a peg or two was always going excite the Millwall ranks; while for the Hammers it was a rare chance to put their noisy neighbours in their place.

The potential for trouble was spotted by the Football League, who asked West Ham to reduce the ticket allocation for visiting fans from 10% capacity to 5%. This meant a mere 1,500 Millwall fans would be allowed into Upton Park on the night, supposedly making life easier for those in charge. The counterview was that the fewer fans you had in the ground, under the watchful eye of police and stewards, the more you had roaming the streets outside.

Whatever the night held, I had eight days to prepare myself for it.

The first thing I had to do was request the afternoon off from work. Happily, my line manager was well-disposed towards what she called my 'hobby'. That's not how I saw it. Officiating at an important match in front of 25,000 critical and vocal fans is not quite the same as wandering up and down a railway station jotting down engine numbers. But there was no need to cloud our relationship with semantics, so I asked the question and got the expected answer. Back then, I still worked for Teaching Personnel as a trainer supporting frontline staff with finding supply teachers on a daily basis. But August was the school holidays, so getting a half-day off was not a problem.

In addition to limiting the number of Millwall fans, the powers-that-be took further precautions. Usually, the match officials would drive to the ground separately and park in the spaces reserved for them. But to reduce any possible involvement with the crowds, we were instructed to convene at the Hilton Hotel in Dartford.

For me, this meant overshooting the venue to get to the meet, being driven back some of the way I'd already come and then doing the whole thing again after the match was over. I was destined to cross the Thames four times before I made it home. (And if anyone had told me how late that would be, I wouldn't have believed them.)

My three colleagues were Paul Taylor, the referee, and Mike George and Neil Hair were my fellow assistant referees. Mike would be running the line with me, while Neil was the fourth official. I hadn't met any of them before, but we were all experienced enough to be trusted with this potentially challenging game. We bonded over a quick cup of coffee and then reached for our standard-issue wheelie bags and marched out to our people carrier, looking in our matching suits as smart and as organised as an aircraft cabin crew. (We were certainly in for some turbulence ahead!)

All was normal until we left the A13 and started threading our way down to Upton Park. Looking out of the windows, you could see the match day build-up: unusual numbers of people milling around; a waving of club favours; snatches of football chants. The atmosphere seeped into our chauffeur-driven bubble. Were we nervous? I wouldn't say that; but we were getting attuned. In only a couple of hours, the four of us would be walking out into a packed stadium to face the full glare of public attention. Of course, it was the players and the game that the thousands of fans were coming to watch. But none of us were under any illusions: they'd be on our case, abusing us for any perceived mistakes on a wildly partisan basis.

As we got closer to the ground, we noticed that the shops had either closed or were closing. Shopkeepers who had metal shutters had pulled them down. Others had boarded up their premises. More dramatically, the statue commemorating the legendary West Ham trio of World Cup winners –Moore, Peters and Hurst – had also been boxed up, as though awaiting relocation to a new plinth.

'Look at all the bizzies!' someone said. And there did seem to be more police than usual.

We eased our way through the crowd and swung into the main entrance. We dropped our kit bags in the match officials' changing room, getting the usual polite greetings from members of the home staff. Then it was time to walk out into the arena. I'd been to Upton Park before – as a fan. You get a very different perspective from the pitch. This is the playing area, the gladiatorial arena and the focal point for the super-charged emotions of several thousand fanatical fans.

> " Trouble had been building throughout the day.

To be part of the officiating team is, of course, a huge privilege. But you really have to be on your game to avoid attracting the attentions of the crowd. And it's not only the crowd watching your every move. The match assessor will be watching every move you make, every step you take. We had Colin Hills, and he came over to introduce himself.

As did the Metropolitan match commander to tell us there were 500 police on duty, with more available if needed. Trouble had been building throughout the day, starting with an incident in Canning Town as early as 10.30am. His officers had been dealing with similar events ever since, which was not surprising with so many supporters in the area necking endless lagers in the summer sunshine. My impression was that the police were on top of things but might be stretched if things escalated. The match commander signed off by telling us the Millwall fans who had tickets were being kettled in a few local pubs before being escorted into the ground just before kick-off. Over to you, gentlemen!

> Paul decided we'd had enough evening air.

There was a bit of time to fill before we needed to change into our kit and do our pre-match warm-up. Enough time to let the nerves build up. Which is probably why Paul said, 'Let's take in the night air,' before leading us not just off the pitch, but out of the ground altogether. This doesn't usually happen, and probably wouldn't have been approved of. But we had nothing better to do, and Paul was our leader, so we followed him through the gates to see what was going on.

It was the familiar pre-match scene, with programme sellers doing a lively trade and other hawkers shouting their wares in evening air heavy with the smell of cooking oil and vinegar. It was noisy, with snatches of chants, boisterous banter and a lot of laughter: atmospheric, but you wouldn't have said hostile or threatening.

But then, from half a mile away, at Upton Park tube station there came an uglier groundswell: more aggressive shouting, the odd siren, and police orders rasped through a megaphone. If trouble hadn't reached the ground, it wasn't far away.

Paul decided we'd had enough evening air and led us back inside the ground.

Four big kit bags open on the benches; four sets of black shorts and shirts; and four pairs of black socks laid out. We'd gauged the state of the turf on our earlier pitch inspection, so each of us chose the appropriate pair of black boots with the right studs. Mike and I got our flags out and unrolled them; Neil checked his notebook and pens; and Paul checked his two watches, his red and yellow cards, and, of course, his whistle. All four of us fitted our earpieces and checked our little intercom system, which would keep us in touch throughout the match.

When the captains – Scott Parker for West Ham and Andy Frampton for Millwall – knocked on the door to deliver their team sheets, Paul was the one leading the pep talk about keeping the game clean and reminding them that the players had a responsibility to conduct themselves well – especially in such a highly charged game as this.

There was one more stage before we were ready for kick-off: the warm-up. Everybody takes the players' warm-up for granted. Out they go with members of the coaching staff to do their little sprints in between the cones and practise rapid-fire passing. But the officials need to stretch their legs and prepare for their hour-and-a-half running up and down as well. You don't want to be haring along the touchline and feel your hamstring go.

So out we went and found a section of the pitch away from the two squads of players who were already there to do our brief routine. The atmosphere was building. The seats weren't full, but there was a steady stream of fans making their way down the rows. It was loud, but nothing like as loud as it would get.

The first thing to turn the volume up was the arrival of the 1,500 Millwall fans. It was like the first appearance of the pantomime villain – a role they had made their own over the years. They were ushered into the Trevor Brooking Stand, hooted and booed from all sides and responding in kind.

Talk of entering the lion's den.

> This was a long-anticipated showdown.

There was a demarcation zone of empty seats heading into the corner where the nearest West Ham fans were seated. It was guarded by a phalanx of yellow-jacketed stewards supported by a few police officers. But the two sets of supporters were close enough to get their messages across, and the tension was there from the start. I'd been to enough football matches to clock that this wasn't going to be a nice family occasion on a warm late summer evening. This was a long-anticipated showdown, and the Millwall fans were far from being daunted by being a heavily outnumbered minority. Not a bit of it. They had plenty to say.

Their familiar taunting cry – 'No one likes us, we don't care!' – rang out loud and clear, along with suggestions as to where the home supporters could lodge their signature bubbles, plus much else beyond the bounds of euphemism. As the AR designated to patrol that end of the pitch, I would have a wall of noise behind me throughout the match.

I could feel my stress levels rising and took this moment of calm before the storm to properly focus on my responsibilities throughout the game. The stand I was going to be sprinting up and down in front of was known as the Chicken Run, and it was crammed to the rafters with home supporters who had the Millwall sector close at hand to their right. Mike would be on the near side running the line in front of the main stand and technical area. Three sides of the ground were packed with West Ham supporters. To say the place was heaving would be an understatement.

The players jogged off, followed by their coaches with their cones, and we also returned to our changing room for the last few minutes before the kick-off. The waiting was the worst part. We knew we were likely to be in for a rough night and we just wanted to get on with it. It must have been pretty tense in the players' changing rooms as well, though at least they wouldn't have thousands of baying fanatics breathing down their necks. But the match could only start at the appointed time, and we sat there looking at Paul, who, as the referee, would determine when we got up and walked out onto the pitch. Eventually, he looked at his watch and, with a nod to the three of us, stood up and led us out to face the music.

The noise hits you as soon as you leave the changing room, distant thunder smashing around the stadium, getting louder with every step. As we walk towards the light at the end of the tunnel, we start to distinguish the various layers of sound. There's the West Ham anthem – 'Forever blowing bubbles...' – crackling over the tannoy, supported by the massed choir of home supporters, while the Millwall fans do their best to drown it in a tide of jeering and abuse.

I happen to be standing in front of the Millwall players in the pre-match formation, and one of them is aggressively geeing up his teammates, saying how badly they are going to piss off the home fans. The teams then pass in front of us so we can shake hands with the players. You don't catch their eyes. No one is mates with anybody at this stage, and we each know that within minutes there'll be Paul's whistle and our flags spoiling it for one side or the other.

We join Paul and the two captains for the coin toss in the centre circle. A handshake and a nod, and the captains trot back to their teams to prepare for the kick-off. Paul stays near the circle, Mike and I run off in opposite directions.

The home fans in the Chicken Run are in full voice. There's a tidal wave of noise from behind me, some of it doubtless cheeky if not downright rude.

But I'm now in my zone. I have to put everything out of my mind and simply concentrate on my responsibilities. Paul checks that everybody is ready, which includes me and Mike, and then blows the whistle.

We're off.

CHAPTER CHALLENGES ANSWERS

1. *No goal – award an indirect free kick to the defending team, as the penalty taker has played the ball twice without the ball touching another player.*

2. *No – they must be a minimum of one yard away from the wall until the kick is taken.*

CHAPTER 8

'If we leave, we won't be coming back'

The Riot of Upton Park, Part 2

Considering the shambles we ended up with, what's surprising looking back is how relatively straightforward the game was. There were no contentious issues, controversial decisions, dodgy offside calls – the sort of thing that can easily inflame an already impassioned situation. The fact that Millwall scored first certainly gave it edge and excitement, but the West Ham faithful had no one to blame but their own defenders. And even Paul's penalty award deep into the match couldn't be faulted. All four match officials had a pretty good game.

CHAPTER CHALLENGES

1. *What is the minimum number of players in a team for a match to start or continue?*

2. *Can a player take a throw-in with just one hand on the ball?*

And so, to be fair, did the players. It was tough, physical football, as befits an English cup tie. You can think that the majority of the foreign players who come into English domestic football on a handsome salary don't quite 'get' derby games, and there's some truth in that. But home-grown players, especially with a local background, certainly do. Scott Parker definitely wanted to win, and so did Andy Frampton for Millwall. But unlike some derby games, which start hard and descend into thuggery, there was very little foul play.

Understandably, having got their early goal, Millwall were intent on defending the lead. The longer they managed to do that, the more frustrating the evening became for the West Ham supporters. And the more fun it became for the Millwall faithful.

1-0 at half time: the perfect match for the neutral. It's always more exciting when the underdogs get ahead – and of course, as the minutes ticked down, the away end got noisier and noisier.

'No one likes us, we don't care!' the Millwall fans yelled. There wasn't much the West Ham supporters behind me could do apart from shout back.

Their team was trailing, and it did look as though we'd be going on into extra time and possibly penalties. The Hammers were mounting wave after wave of attacks at the goal and were frustrated every time by stubborn defending or inaccurate shooting.

With about ten minutes to go, I noticed some scuffling between supporters and stewards. A few of the West Ham fans seemed to be trying to invade the pitch, though what good they thought that could do was beyond me. Play seemed to be stuck in my quarter of the ground, with West Ham keeping the pressure up but with nothing to show for it. The noise was off the scale, and our officials' intercom was barely loud enough for us to communicate. When we did, we had to yell.

I was hovering in line with the penalty area, and I could see things getting out of hand with both sets of supporters. The Millwall lot were plunging towards the demarcation zone with the clear intention of mixing it with the home fans who were now struggling to break through the barrier formed by the stewards. I could see the police contingent being reinforced.

At this point, someone threw a bottle onto the pitch. That could have been the spark, but it didn't hit anybody, and Paul didn't make much of it – just stooped to pick it up and lob it to one of the stewards.

And then it happened. With only a few minutes of the second half left, West Ham equalised. I was a matter of yards away and had no reason to raise my flag either for offside or foul play, which in the circumstances was extremely good news.

> The last thing they wanted was to invite a pitch invasion.

Everybody went wild, and the West Ham players, having worked so hard to get the goal, deserved their moment of celebration. It's just a shame they chose my corner of the ground to celebrate in. I am quite sure that the last thing they wanted was to invite a pitch invasion. But in the excitement of the moment, that's what they got. West Ham fans broke through the stewards' cordon and sprinted towards their heroes.

I now realised there were fans leaping over the barrier from the Chicken Run behind me. Completely out of order, but there was no point doing a King Canute and trying to turn back the tide. And I certainly didn't want to be caught up in it. The last thing you want is to lose your footing in a stampede. The only sensible option was to trot towards the centre circle.

The majority of the West Ham fans were celebrating rather than threatening violence, and the first thing many of them did once they were on the pitch was to take selfies on their phones. This wasn't the smartest thing to do. Just by being on the pitch they were in danger of jeopardising the continuation of the match and risking personal sanctions as punishment. But their next move – to run towards the Millwall fans – was particularly dumb. The last thing the evening needed was a mass punch-up between the two sets of supporters.

By this time, the players were heading for the centre circle as though by common consent. I thought staying on the pitch was the right thing to do. Anyway, it was Paul's decision, so I joined him and Mike and waited to see if security could clear the playing area so the game could be finished.

Their first priority was obviously stopping the clash between home and away fans. Had that failed, there would have been a bloodbath. Letting the idiots run around the pitch was a far preferable option.

But it was still not good. Especially not for the home club. Pitch invasions are taken very seriously, and clubs can be penalised with fines – or worse. If the game couldn't be restarted, it would have to be replayed. Or even cancelled, with the win awarded to Millwall. Having just got themselves back in the match with their late equaliser, it was in West Ham's best interests to clear the pitch and let the game restart.

The players themselves did their level best to persuade their fans to go back to the stands. They didn't want to be slapped on the back or have their hands shaken. They just wanted the opportunity to finish the job and get through to the next round.

Although the match was not being screened live, there were Sky cameras present, and the footage that I saw later showed one bare-chested fan running down the middle of the pitch towards the Millwall supporters, giving some pretty unambiguous hand gestures.

The tannoy was barking orders for people to return to their seats, appealing to the home crowds' better instincts and issuing dire threats to those who didn't comply. The police were already hauling a few offenders off to face criminal charges – and possible life-bans from the club.

Paul, Mike and I stayed in our little huddle. All three of us were relieved there had been no questions about the validity of the West Ham goal. Offside would have been an unpleasant call for me to have had to make at that stage in the game.

After a while, order was restored. The would-be combatants were kept apart and the last stragglers were shooed off the pitch back to their stands. The players spread to their starting positions, Mike and I jogged back to our respective lines, and Paul was able to blow his whistle for the restart.

Play resumed for barely five minutes. Neil held up the added time, but there had been so few stops in play that that only amounted to a couple of minutes (Paul had stopped his watch for the duration of the pitch invasion). Neither side wanted to risk losing the tie in the sliver of time left, and both teams were relieved when Paul blew the whistle to bring the first act of the drama to a close, with the score remaining 1-1.

Everybody stayed on the pitch. Managers and coaches ran on for a quick word, and water bottles were handed out. But the policy is to keep the momentum up, so it's really just a short interlude before the two 15-minute halves which should produce the result. If it doesn't, it's penalties.

The only formality is a second toss to determine ends, and for this Neil Harris and Rob Green joined Scott Parker and Andy Frampton in the centre circle. The relationship between the players was excellent. They were on the same side in wanting good, competitive football uninterrupted by the fans. There was certainly no belligerence between the two teams. If anything, they seemed as bemused as anyone about the heightened atmosphere the game had generated.

It wasn't long before the deadlock was broken. Paul awarded a penalty for an undeniable handball in the box after a great signal from Mike, and Junior Stanislas slotted home from the spot to give West Ham the lead, 2-1. This was enough for the vast majority of the West Ham fans. But not the minority. There was another pitch invasion, with one guy in a blue hooped T-shirt running all the way to the centre circle flicking V-signs at the Millwall players. You'd need to be a psychiatrist to unravel the mindset of someone prepared to risk a fine or a banning order for a snatch of the limelight like that.

> " If anything they seemed as bemused as anyone.

The Millwall players didn't rise to the bait but, at a nod from their captain, walked with great dignity off the pitch to the technical area. At 2-1, it would be to their advantage if the game were abandoned. To their credit, they didn't carry on down the tunnel to their changing room. They simply stood around waiting. The West Ham players also left the pitch and similarly stood in a group around their manager.

We officials stayed out there, once more in the centre circle. As Paul said, 'If we leave, we won't be coming back.' We made it clear we were ready to continue the match once the pitch invaders had been cleared from the playing area. Which was certainly what the majority of the crowd wanted.

There was loud booing from the stands and shouts for people to get off and stop spoiling it for everybody else.

The situation was looking increasingly grim, with the offenders playing tag with the stewards and police. Gianfranco Zola, West Ham's manager, decided to intervene and stepped out across the grass to appeal to the delinquent fans and urge them back to their seats. At the same time, some were walking brazenly up to the players and demanding joint selfies. They didn't get them. No one wanted to have anything to do with them.

Eventually, the herding cats exercise succeeded in clearing the pitch and the game could continue. Three sides of the ground were expansively vocal, cheering on their team, while the Millwall end was subdued as the visiting fans sensed the chance of beating their local rivals was slipping away.

This was confirmed when West Ham scored again in the first half of extra time. 3-1. There was just time for a bare-chested pitch invader to leap out from the Chicken Run waving his shirt above his head as though he'd just scored the winning goal. Once more the stewards set off in pursuit, eventually capturing him and marching him off.

The Millwall fans had accepted defeat by this stage – but not gracefully. They started ripping up their seats and started chucking them at the long-suffering security personnel. Talk about chucking your toys out of the pram.

Extra time, second half. Millwall couldn't make up the lost ground, and the Hammers were content to take it easy, keeping the ball safe and not risking getting caught on the break. The final whistle came as a relief to everyone.

The stadium announcer appealed for calm, asking people not to come onto the pitch again, but a sizeable number ignored him and burst through the stewards once more to throng around the players. They were not amused. Rob Green, the England and West Ham goalkeeper, was clearly disgusted. Pushing through the throng of supporters, he made a point of congratulating the Millwall players for their gutsy performance before stomping off down the tunnel without any acknowledgement of the home fans' cheers. I could see the Millwall players were tempted to trot over to thank their supporters in the Trevor Brooking Stand but, with West Ham fans still running loose on the pitch, thought better of it.

Paul, Mike and I shook hands with the players, and both teams appreciated that we'd conducted things as well as we could given the circumstances. Failure on our part could have made the evening a hell of a lot worse.

Although we had played our part, we still had to hang around in our changing room for quite a while as word filtered through of more trouble inside and outside the stadium. The police had to kettle the Millwall supporters to get them away from the area, and there were running battles on Green Street and all the way up to the tube station.

Eventually, we got the signal to return to our people carrier and, under a heavy police escort, we followed the Millwall team bus away out of the danger zone. After a while, we slipped away back to Dartford to pick up our cars for the journey home, which, for me, meant yet another Thames crossing. It would be many long hours before I got to my front door. I let myself in at 2.30am but was still too hyper to sleep. Instead, I sent an email to the Football League referee manager, Dave Allison, thanking him for the game. I meant that sincerely. It had been an epic day, and there were moments when I really did feel my life was on the line, but for sheer excitement there was nothing to match it.

Normality resumed with the alarm clock set for 6.30am, and I slipped off to work, arriving on the dot of 8.00. 'What the –?' was the first response of colleagues when I walked into the office, with my line manager, Rachel, raising her eyebrows knowingly. An hour later, the call from home came. In my effort not to stir things up in the small hours, I had replied to Jacqueline's sleepy query of 'How was the match?' with a whispered 'Very quiet'. Suffice it to say, the phone conversation was anything but. I had only just persuaded Jacqueline that my life hadn't really been at risk when the MD called me into his office.

This usually meant trouble, but as he shut the door behind me, he grinned broadly and said, 'Tell me about last night.' So I did. And continued to repeat it throughout the day. My 'hobby' had never attracted much interest or respect, but being there on television in the midst of a riot certainly got a few people's attention.

Later, Dave Allison called to thank me and to praise the officiating quartet for doing what they could to quell the storm. I assured him we were all okay and praised Paul for his assured leadership. Inevitably, the papers and politicians were vocal in their condemnation of the two sets of fans in what had looked like a return to the bad old days of the seventies and eighties. The football authorities immediately instigated an investigation with a view to punishing both clubs. The charge list included violent, threatening and provocative behaviour, and the use of obscene and racist language. West Ham were also charged with failing to prevent their supporters encroaching on the field of play. I was one of the many witnesses interviewed by the FA and simply gave as accurate account of what I'd seen as I could.

A lot of the trouble took place in the streets around the ground, and it was apparent that much of it had been premeditated. The Metropolitan Police launched Operation Balconi to look into this aspect of the event, and 80 people suspected of violence before and after the match were arrested.

In their hunt for culprits, the police released a gallery of 66 people they wanted to talk to, some appearing on the BBC's *Crimewatch* programme. Several West Ham supporters were found guilty of violent disorder, and some were sent to prison, including one for 20 months. Many received banning orders, and West Ham banned at least 54 people from the ground for life, 11 of them season ticket holders. The club itself was fined £115,000 for the behaviour of their supporters and for failing to prevent them getting onto the pitch.

And that was the Riot of Upton Park, 25th August 2009.

CHAPTER CHALLENGES ANSWERS

1. *Seven – one of whom must be a goalkeeper. If one team has five players sent off, the match is abandoned.*

2. *No – Law says that both hands must be used to throw the ball. Also, you cannot use one hand to throw the ball and the other to 'guide' it.*

PART 3

WITHIN TOUCHING
DISTANCE?

CHAPTER 9

No Time to be Starstruck

Me, Roy Keane, Paulo Di Canio and a Bollocking from Mark Noble

Upton Park was always going to be the stand-out match of the 2009/10 season, but I was becoming used to big occasions and to seeing big-name players close up. With some trepidation, I ran the line in another Millwall match, an FA Cup third-round replay against Derby County, but the only trouble I had was keeping warm on a viciously cold January evening. The great thing about being an assistant referee is you are guaranteed anonymity. No one pays you any attention – until you make a mistake – and then they're only shouting abuse at your back. Not one of the Millwall supporters would have given me a second glance. It was just the threat of chilblains that worried me – though that was mitigated by seeing Robbie Savage live for the first time. He was brilliant. Typically, the match went to penalties, meaning it lengthened the time we spent out on the pitch. I was quietly pleased when it was all over and we could get warm again in the dressing room.

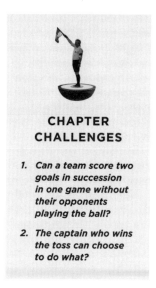

CHAPTER CHALLENGES

1. *Can a team score two goals in succession in one game without their opponents playing the ball?*

2. *The captain who wins the toss can choose to do what?*

By the following season, I was feeling pretty well adjusted to life as a League official – the quality of the play, the size of the stadiums and the thunderous noise of the crowd. I mixed with well-known players and managers and felt confident in myself. But some encounters you can't prepare for. In August 2010, I was appointed junior assistant referee for the Championship game between Crystal Palace and Ipswich Town. As the junior, it was my job to knock on the door of the away team's dressing room and conduct the kit check on the players. This was something I'd done many times before and I felt fine when I made the call to get the Ipswich players into the tunnel to inspect their boots and make sure they were wearing the right strips with the correct numbers on. I was expecting the captain to open the door but instead found myself looking the Ipswich manager Roy Keane straight in the eye.

> " A month or so later there was no escape.

Arguably the most formidable player of the modern era (with some very old-school ways of making his intentions clear), Keane was somebody you really didn't want to get on the wrong side of, and a face-to-face encounter made me feel vulnerable and anxious, even though I hadn't done anything wrong and he was already looking over his shoulder, calling his team to line up and follow me down the corridor to be inspected. I could only imagine what it would be like to be confronted by him in the heat of battle and very glad that I would be on the opposite side of the pitch from the technical area during the match.

A month or so later, there was no escape. I was the fourth official in a match between Queens Park Rangers and Doncaster Rovers and so was rooted to the technical area, where I revisited my relationship with Neil Warnock, manager of the home team. QPR were really finding some form and played well. However, that didn't make their manager any less sensitive to perceived errors on the part of the referee, whose representative I was. Time and time again, either Neil or his assistant, Keith Curle, demanded I queried decisions over the communication system.

After a while, this persistent questioning became unacceptable. The referee had better things to do than justify what he had done while trying to make sure his next call was the correct one – as he explained to me in no uncertain terms at half time. After the restart, the demand for justification continued, so I simply told Neil that comms were down and I couldn't get through to the ref. He and Curle reverted to hand-waving and shouting. They can't have had much to complain about, as QPR trounced the visitors 3-0.

All managers are different. What they share is a passionate commitment to their teams, which can translate into a one-eyed view of every decision made by officials. In their defence, they are all under intense pressure. They are judged by their teams' performances, which in the fans' view can always be improved. By definition, at least six teams in every league will be in danger of relegation come the second half of a season; and even if your team is top of the Premier Division at Christmas, you're still going to be looking over your shoulder and worrying that you'll drop points and let your rivals back in. It is a statistical truism that the majority of clubs in all the leagues will have a disappointing season – certainly judged by the inflated expectation of their fans.

In November 2010, I was fourth official again in yet another Millwall game – at home to Sheffield United. When I felt a tap on my shoulder just before kick-off, I may have swung around slightly aggressively to see what the problem was. But there wasn't a problem – just Gary Speed, the Sheffield manager, offering his hand and wishing me well for the game. I was really touched that someone of his standing, who had a really big 90 minutes before him, took time to acknowledge that I too had my role to play and was likely to be a bit nervous. The magnitude of that small gesture was even more meaningful when I heard the news less than a year later that Gary had taken his own life at the tragically young age of 42.

That same month, I was junior assistant referee for a match between Sheffield Wednesday and Walsall, venue: Hillsborough. As I ran towards the Leppings Lane end to check the net before kick-off, my mind was on the fateful day 20 years before when nearly a hundred Liverpool fans lost their lives just a few yards away in the crush of the overcrowded stands. I stood for a moment's contemplation and then trotted over to my line, ready to do my absolute best by the players and spectators of the game ahead.

> " My mind was on the fateful day twenty years before.

For all the tragedies, scandals and outrages that make the front pages and call forth denunciations from pundits and commentators, English football is without question a power for good. Every week, hundreds of thousands of people attend hundreds of matches, League and non-League, up and down the country, cheering on their teams, taking pleasure in the amazing skills on display – even from opponents – and go home uplifted, excited, reconciled to their mundane lives. The tiny minority who draw all the attention are just that – a tiny minority, selfish, stupid and unwanted. For the vast majority, and for the millions that watch on television, the game is still beautiful and inspiring. And it is great to be a tiny cog in the well-oiled machine that guarantees that every match is officiated to the highest possible standard.

I was always trying to raise my own standard by breaking new ground, and the following season saw me driving down to Bournemouth in August 2011 for my first game involving a Premier League team. West Bromwich Albion were the visitors. It was a League Cup match, but WBA brought the sparkle of the Premiership with them, and I was excited. As the senior assistant referee, I would be patrolling the line in front of the technical area and would be scrutinised by Roy Hodgson, who was WBA's manager at the time. Roy was one of the more progressive and cerebral of the home-grown managers. An English Arsène Wenger if you like. Certainly, someone I deeply respected, and I hoped to his catch pearls of wisdom as I ran the line. There may have been some tactical gems, but quite often he fell back on the classic roar of 'Clear it!' heard from all managers at moments of crisis. Roy was as charming as I'd expected, and he went home satisfied with a comfortable 4-1 victory.

I followed that with a game that gave a turbocharged boost to my career on the National List. It was a Football League Championship match in September 2011 between West Ham United and Portsmouth, and so I was back at Upton Park. The match was live on television for an Asian audience, with extended highlights that evening on the BBC. The turn-out at the ground was 33,465 – so it was a big game. As senior AR, I was on the near touchline in front of the main stand, so I was going to be in the eye of the critical storm from both the home supporters and the technical area, where Sam Allardyce would be looking out for West Ham, while Steve Cotterill would be equally critical on behalf of Portsmouth.

It was a cracking match, end-to-end stuff with goals for both sides. The first half passed without major incident, but in the second half I found myself in the limelight not once but twice. I made two tight decisions in real time. I gave what I saw but was eager to watch the recorded game when I got home and was thrilled to hear Tony Gubba's commentary on both of them.

The first was a handball in the Portsmouth penalty area. Under the intense pressure of a West Ham attack, one of the defenders used his hand. I was the best placed match official to see the offence, though I had thousands of West Ham supporters helpfully roaring '*Handball! Handball!*' behind me. Tony Gubba also saw it: 'Oh, there was a hand!' My only concern was that the player was inside the penalty area, which he was. I looked to the referee, Roger East, who hadn't seen it (or, less likely, hadn't heard the verdict of the home crowd), and as he didn't blow his whistle and point to the spot, it was my duty to raise my flag. 'That might be a penalty,' Gubba remarked. Roger blew the whistle to stop play and find out what I had seen – it might have been offside or a bit of foul play off the ball. But I told him over the comms system that it was handball. 'It's going to be a penalty!' Gubba chirped, and Mark Noble stepped up to score from the spot.

It's a big call for an assistant referee to make – which is why we usually wait for the referee to do the honours. They have the whistle after all. But I was confident I'd got it right and, tellingly, there were no protests from the Portsmouth players or fans. For a while, I was flavour of the month with the

West Ham supporters. But that changed when they witnessed my second intervention. It was very near the end of the game after Carlton Cole had scored the fourth goal for the home side. After the restart, I saw one of the West Ham players, Frédéric Piquionne, clash with an opponent. Piquionne raised his hands to the face of the Portsmouth player, who crashed to the ground. I'd seen the whole incident from start to finish and briefed Roger, who immediately felt in his top pocket and produced a red card. Again, tellingly, there were no boos from the stands. And happily, there were no complaints from the two managers, who came out of a nail-biting encounter (4-3 to West Ham) with their tempers intact.

The match assessor was Paul Alcock and he supported me with both my Key Match Decisions (KMDs). However, I didn't escape without a sanction. I got a decision over a throw-in wrong, and for that I got a very lively bollocking from Mark Noble, much to the delight of the home fans. That wasn't enough to spoil my mark for the match, which pushed me right up the Merit List. It was a fantastic day and one of my best as an AR. I look back at the highlights on YouTube and am reminded of just how good an atmosphere Upton Park

> Maybe they thought we were players.

was able to produce, making up for the horrifying scenes I'd witnessed on its night of shame.

I got confirmation that I was in the assessors' good books when I was picked for duty for an FA Cup third-round tie just after Christmas. That is always a good sign. The match was between West Bromwich Albion and Cardiff City, i.e. a Premier League side versus a Championship side, which gave me the opportunity to work with a Premier League referee, Lee Probert. He was kind, welcoming – and clearly on another level of expertise and presence. All the Premier League officials have that extra something, and as I wanted to join them at the very top, I always savoured the chance to work with them. It was a good game, which WBA won 4-2. So, plenty of goals and the home supporters very happy.

Two months later, I was officiating in a match between Chelsea and Manchester United. No, not as a result of a mercurial promotion, alas. It was the FA Youth Cup semi-final second leg, so the only TV it was on was the Chelsea FC channel. But still, it was a good day out, and a rare chance to involve my son, Sam, an ardent Chelsea fan. I took him onto the pitch with me for the pre-match inspection and we got waved to by a tour group looking on from the Shed End. Maybe they thought we were players. Anyway, it was nice showing Sam what I was doing with my time when I wasn't at home with the family. It ended 1-1, so he at least had the satisfaction of not seeing his team lose.

There was arguably more at stake in a League 2 match later in the spring. Swindon Town travelled to Aldershot needing just one point to clinch promotion. I was the senior assistant – in front of the main stand and the technical area – and given the amount resting on the game, it was never going to be a stroll in the park. The visitors' end was packed with Swindon fans roaring their team on, and the Shots were their usual stubborn selves, never happier than when frustrating the ambitions of a supposedly bigger and better club. They scored the opening goal, though that was not the most significant thing that happened in the first half as far as I was concerned.

The referee, Mark Heywood, came onto the comms to flag up a suspected pulled hamstring. He seemed to be moving okay and said he would try to run it off. But at half time, he conceded that his match was over. Mine was about to get a great deal more interesting. As the senior AR, I would be taking over. For 45 minutes, I was going to be a Football League referee – something I'd dreamed of for years.

The tannoy announcement confirmed my new status; the fourth official dug out his flag and I dug out my whistle and my red and yellow cards and checked my watch was functioning. And then off we went into the second half. I loved it. What nerves I had were soon blown away by the intensity of the game. Things moved at a blistering pace, and I had to run all over the pitch keeping up with the action. But the skill level of the players was so high that it made reading the game surprisingly easy. You could see where the centre-half was intending to pass, and then, instead of under-hitting it or shanking it into the stands, the ball arrived at the winger's feet, and I'd already be running hard to monitor what happened next.

Being in the right place at the right time is vital, especially when it comes to awarding a penalty. And, yes, I did have to give a penalty when one of the Aldershot defenders used his hand, and that did result in Swindon clawing their way back into the game. But the Shots supporters made no complaint – they just urged their team to keep fighting and get their noses back in front again. They put in a gutsy performance and the whole game was pretty robust. I reached for my yellow card three times – again, without much dissent – and when the home side did get their second goal, it was all about holding on till the end of the match. There were three minutes of added time, and they seemed to take forever as Swindon pushed hard for the equaliser. But at last my watch told me to blow the final whistle, which triggered a tidal wave of applause from the home crowd.

So, no promotion for Swindon – at least not that day. But no hard feelings either; although, when their manager, Paolo Di Canio, walked towards us at the end, he looked extremely disappointed. However, he was a real gentleman and said simply '*Grazie*' as he shook our hands before turning to Swindon's fans and acknowledging their support.

It had all happened so quickly; I was still trying to come to terms with what I had done as we sat in our changing room sharing a pizza. I felt I had passed the test. No one questioned my decisions, even if they hadn't liked them, and I hadn't missed anything as far as I was concerned. I was pleased with myself but acknowledged that my build-up for the game would have been completely different if I had known I was going to referee it. This way I hadn't really had time to get nervous.

Would I ever get the chance again?

That would depend, in part, on a decision I was asked to make for the 2012/13 season.

There were big changes in the PGMOL and FA organisations from this season onwards, resulting in a stronger distinction between those who operated in the Premier League, the Select Group of officials, and the National List referees who operated in the Football League. Now, a new group of specialist assistant referees was introduced. These would be by invitation only and would require those selected to dedicate themselves to the AR role and commit to working exclusively for the Football League. I was one of those invited to be on the SAR list.

It was an honour, and I was pleased to be asked. But it was also the glass ceiling for my career. As it more or less said on the tin, I would be confirmed as a top official – but in the second tier of the football pyramid. Dreams of moving into the Premier League would have to be abandoned – along with progressing as a referee.

Possibly as a result of my stepping into the breach the previous season, I had been promoted to a Level 2b referee, which theoretically meant I could ref at a higher level than before. But that higher level was a lot lower than the level at which I would be picked as AR. Time to take stock and come to a decision. I was now 42, and age counts against you in football, as in so many walks of life. I could still do the job – I wouldn't have still been there if I couldn't pass the fitness tests every year – but up against an equally qualified colleague who had ten years less on the clock? It was obvious who they would choose. I had to be realistic, and it seemed foolish to turn down the new – and prestigious – appointment to sustain a fantasy of making it to the Premiership as a referee. So I accepted the invitation, attended the PGMOL conference, where I collected my new kit and devoted the summer to making sure I passed the all-important fitness test.

My first game was a pre-season friendly between MK Dons and Fulham. I was fourth official, which wasn't a bad option on a hot August evening. One of my duties was to deal with substitutions. I had to check the players for jewellery, make sure their studs were safe, confirm their shirt number tallied with what I had on the team sheet. A few things to think about, but not too complicated when you're used to it.

I got notification from the MK Dons' bench saying they wanted to make a substitution, but I couldn't see anyone getting ready to come on and received no indication of who was coming off, so I went to the technical area to find out who it would be. That season, MK Dons had appointed Ian Wright to be their coach, and he proved to be another famous person it was a joy to meet in real life. I asked him, 'Who do you want to take off?' Without a pause for thought, he replied, 'Fulham's number 7 – he's killing us down the right-hand side.'

I was still laughing five minutes later.

I wasn't laughing later in the season when I was again the fourth official. As I've just said, it's not an onerous job. There are only a few things you have to do. But organising a substitution is a lot more challenging when you've left the electronic number board in the changing room, especially on a ground where the dressing rooms are on the opposite side of the pitch to the technical area. This was exactly the scenario at Brentford's old ground, Griffin Park. There was no way I could quickly run and get it. I'd have been a laughingstock. The substitution went ahead without the board. Most people wouldn't have noticed, but I knew one person who would: the assessor. And although I pleaded with a reluctant steward to go and get it for me so I could flag up the extra time at the end of the first half, and made no further errors, I was left in no doubt I had committed a cardinal sin.

I was looking forward to the assessor's debrief like a schoolboy caught truanting waiting to be seen by the headmaster, but he was generous. 'Gavin,' he said, 'I didn't see you raise the number board at the first substitution.' Statement of fact with a strongly implied question. 'No, you didn't,' I replied. Agreement with statement of fact and implicit acceptance of guilt. It was very tactfully handled. Quite rightly, my assessment report included developmental advice and my mark reflected the mistake I had made.

But by April the following year, that minor blot on my copybook had obviously been expunged. I was having a good season and my marks were high. I was given Nottingham Forest v Blackpool, and in addition to the compliment of a Championship fixture, I had the joy of officiating at a ground that had once been home to Brian Clough's European Champions of 1979 and 1980. I loved being on the pitch of such a famous stadium, thinking of all the greats who had played there over the years.

The referee was Craig Pawson, who was also having a good season. It was obvious that this was a 'development' game for him. In other words, if he impressed, it would prove he was good enough for the final step up to the Premier League. Maybe that was the case with me too, I thought. Craig was great to work with. Sometimes, you just click with someone and it makes the job so much easier.

But being in sync with your referee won't guarantee you an easy passage with the team managers and coaches. On this occasion, I was the senior AR, so spent a lot of time near the technical area. Behind me was Paul Ince of Blackpool, along with Alex Rae. I was bombarded with questions – not always easy to answer when you're concentrating on what's happening now rather than analysing something that happened a minute or two ago.

> 66 I had committed a cardinal sin.

Normally, if a manager asks questions, it's because they're not happy about a decision the officials have made. I did my best, but whether Paul was happy with my answers I don't know. He didn't say. Half the time I'd be haring off down the line following play. I'm not saying he was harbouring negative thoughts about how we were running the match. He was really very pleasant. It's just that running the line may look as though that's all you have to do; but you have to concentrate on every second of the game, so being constantly asked questions can be distracting.

But it was a good game, and the debrief was very positive. Craig had done well, as had I, and I drove home happy. At the end of the season, Craig was promoted to the Select Group, and that meant he would be on the Premier League list the following season. No such news for me. I felt I was close; but not quite close enough.

Maybe another high-profile game right at the end of the season played a part? This was Swindon Town v Brentford in the Football League 1 play-off semi-final first leg. This appointment was further proof that I had been going really well, and another opportunity to show I was too good to be overlooked for promotion. I was full of excitement and enthusiasm when I arrived – looking forward to a good game in which to exhibit the high standard I had reached.

But sometimes circumstances conspire against you. The referee was Tony Harrington and this was the first time we'd met. I obviously tried to do all the right things and to work well with him, but we just didn't click. I couldn't get things right, and at one key moment we signalled the opposite way from each other. It happens, but it deflated me and left me feeling miserable.

The timing of the game and the condition of the pitch were also against me. Sky was broadcasting the match live, which dictated a late afternoon kick-off (5pm). This meant that I had bright sunshine coming in low straight into my eyes for the whole match. Have you ever seen a linesman wearing a cap or dark glasses? No, you haven't. It's not allowed. I struggled to see the play and had to shield my eyes with my free hand. You try that while running to keep up with a winger as fit as a thoroughbred horse. And you've not only got to keep up with him but with where the defenders are when he received the ball so as to judge whether he's offside or not.

Because we were in one of those early summer droughts making the ground hard as concrete, the pitch had been heavily watered to help the players. But it didn't help me as there was too much water along the line, turning it into a mud bath. Nothing I could do about where I had to put my feet, but it meant my acceleration was slow and my sprinting laboured. As for the linesman's signature sidestepping, I felt I was lifting my feet out of glue.

The game was a 1-1 draw, so nothing I'd done had spoilt it for either team or their supporters. But it was spoilt for me because I felt my performance was below par for reasons that I had no control over. Which was a shame, as this was another high-profile opportunity to show what I could do.

I was not appointed to a play-off game again.

CHAPTER CHALLENGES ANSWERS

1. *Yes – they score with the last kick of the first half, then take kick-off at the start of the second half and score again without conceding possession of the ball.*

2. *They can choose ends or choose to kick off. If they choose to kick off, then the other captain can choose ends.*

CHAPTER 10

The Long and Winding Road

Nearly There

M25, M3, A303, A30, A38. For example. And then back, of course. No worse than a travelling salesman (if they still exist). Except having driven for over three hours, you then had to face the most demanding examination – of your fitness, your experience, your knowledge of the game – in front of a passionate and partisan crowd, to be signed off by a coldly dispassionate assessor, who would have picked up on any and every tiny mistake, before climbing back in the car and retracing your way home. Every weekend from August to May. On top of that, you've got a living to earn through the working week. There's inevitably going to be wear and tear, both physical and mental, and unsatisfactory compromises with work and family. Nothing lasts forever, and I was reminded of that when, for the first time ever, I failed the fitness test. 9am on a hot day in mid-July 2013. It was always going to get hotter, and though I passed the sprints test, I felt drained: fatigued, sick, thirsty. The High Intensity running session was next, and by now the sun was seriously hot.

CHAPTER CHALLENGES

1. *A player is in an offside position but not interfering with play when they are fouled by an opponent. What do you do?*

2. *Can you be penalised for offside in your own half?*

You had to run with the others around the circuit, and I was in trouble after five laps – well off the pace and not covering the required 150m in 30 seconds. I was given a warning after six laps but just couldn't make up the lost ground. After the seventh lap, they pulled me off. I had failed the test.

And without passing, I couldn't officiate. The retest was at the end of July, so no pre-season warm up matches for me. I simply had to focus on getting up to speed for my make-or-break second and last chance on the track.

Thankfully, I passed retest, so was back in the game. I shrugged the failure off – hot day, just wasn't on song. But I knew it was a warning that I was going to find it tough just staying where I was, let alone making it to the higher level I'd been striving for so long.

There was one compensation for my delayed start: I wasn't given a League match on the opening day of the season. This meant I was free to be fourth official in a friendly between Crystal Palace (just back in the top flight) and the legendary Italian club Lazio. A lovely warm August day, great atmosphere, a relaxed but appreciative crowd. And I was working with Phil Dowd, one of the top-ranking referees.

> 66 Non ti preoccupare.

It was a pretty straightforward afternoon for all of us – an uncontroversial 1-0 victory for the visitors. My one regret was that I failed miserably to communicate with the Lazio coaches. What a good impression I would have made if I'd taken the time to mug up one or two phrases. *Non ti preoccupare!* But it was a good way to ease into the season.

Late November. Rather different weather but similar situation. I had not been given an appointment for the Saturday, so decided to catch up on some work around the house before going out for a run. Then I got the SOS call. Dave Allison told me to get in my car immediately and drive to Leicester. Someone had fallen out so needed replacing. And this was not a request: the first qualified official within driving distance is simply told to pack up their kit and get going. Leicester v Millwall. But it was a game, and at least Dave made me feel wanted. I scribbled a hurried note ('Gone to Leicester... See you later') and was on the road in less than 15 minutes.

My kit was washed but it wasn't dry, so as I was making my way up the M1, I was hanging my socks from the mirror with the heater on full. That made me uncomfortably hot but didn't have the desired outcome as far as the socks were concerned. I was late at the ground, but that was allowed under the circumstances. I managed to find a radiator to address the sock problem and was good to go come the 3pm start. I soon stopped fretting about the slightly damp socks and of course completely forgot the afternoon I'd planned and all the little jobs I'd promised to do on my first free afternoon for months. Which probably explained the slightly frosty greeting I received when I got home at 8pm that evening.

April 2014, and we were over the winter and enjoying spring sunshine on our backs. I had a Championship game between QPR and Nottingham Forest. It was live on Sky and also the 25th anniversary of the Hillsborough Disaster. As Forest were playing Liverpool in that FA Cup semi, it made the date particularly poignant. All kick-offs across the country were set for six minutes after the normal time to reflect the 3.06 stoppage back in 1989. The occasion seemed special, and not just for its historical associations. Harry Redknapp was QPR manager and Stuart Pearce was there as the future Forest manager – football royalty.

However, I didn't have any time to bask in reflected glory. I had a job to do, and with only 1 minute and 7 seconds gone, I did it. Yossi Benayoun scored for QPR at my end and all the Forest defenders appealed for offside and stared at me – and at my flag, which remained down. As the initial shot came in, I didn't see Benayoun. He wasn't on my radar. I assumed he must have made a late run, so I kept my flag down and the goal was given.

Immediately, I started to question myself, and I was left in no doubt as to how Forest felt about it. The left-back coming over to take a throw muttered, 'Cost us there, lino,' adding, as he rubbed the ball on his shirt, 'You owe us one now.' That isn't the way it works. Even when you do make a mistake, the only thing you can do is try to put it out of your mind and make sure you remain unbiased. You don't try to compensate by giving something to the aggrieved team, because then you lose the plot completely. But putting it out of your mind is far from easy, especially when there's a huge television audience and the commentators would have slow-motion replays to judge you by. I wouldn't find out until half time whether I'd got it right or not.

When we did traipse off, I caught the eye of one of the Sky team and he winked at me. I had got it right! I could have hugged him. Looking at the replay later, Benayoun was clearly two yards onside. I had judged the flash lag effect perfectly. It was a brilliant decision, as even the disappointed Forest players had to agree. The difference a couple of yards makes.

Not long after – and possibly because of that close call – I was junior AR in the FA Premier League U21 League Cup final between Reading and Manchester City. I certainly took it as a mark of approval and thoroughly enjoyed the occasion. Patrick Viera, another legend, was the Manchester City manager, and at the end of the game, which Reading won 2-0, he came up and thanked the officials, conceding that his side were beaten fair and square.

The event ended up with the usual presentation, so I got a second Premier League medal. If someone had told me when I started out as a referee that I would receive two Premier League medals, an FA medal and a Football League medal in my career, I'd have laughed. But I did, and I have them to this day.

In the summer of 2014, I realised that after six seasons on the National List and two of them as a specialist assistant referee, it was now or never if I was to get promoted to the Select Group. I was 44 and every summer the training I needed to do to pass the fitness test seemed to get a little harder. I still felt at my peak and I was an established figure on the National List, so it was down to me to give it my best shot.

As usual, there were stand-out games or stand-out incidents within games. A Championship derby in August 2014 between Ipswich Town and Norwich City was a lunchtime kick-off shown live on Sky. I had stayed locally the night before, so there were no anxieties about being on time. I had a very relaxed afternoon enjoying a tightly fought game which went to Norwich by a single goal. I was on the main stand side and didn't have much to do. My colleague across the pitch was not so lucky. The goal Norwich scored came as the result of a decision not to call a borderline offside. As far as I could judge – in real time – it was a great call and one that I would have made myself. Unfortunately, under the microscopic freeze-frame analysis of the assessors, it was judged a mistake, and a serious one at that as the result hung on it. I had had no difficult decisions; my colleague got one and got it wrong. I drove home with much the better feedback. Swings and roundabouts as always.

I had another enjoyable and untaxing Championship game in the same month. Fulham were at home to Cardiff City and I was fourth official, which meant that I would have a companionable afternoon with two high-profile managers, Felix Magath (Fulham) and Ole Gunnar Solskjær (Cardiff). Often, big-name managers liked to throw their weight around and engage you in mind games to influence your decisions. But I was in luck with these two, and although my German and Norwegian would barely get me a glass of lager, their English was fluent enough for communication to flow.

I did have occasion to ask Felix to take his seat after he'd leapt up to make a point to his players (the regulations stipulate only two representatives of each team can be standing at a time). There wasn't much you could do if managers refused to respect that, but Felix not only responded immediately, but made a point of apologising to me as he sat down. I thought, 'You've won the European Cup, played in the World Cup finals for Germany and managed Bayern Munich, and now you're apologising to me, an anonymous fourth official, for a trivial breach of the rules! Pretty classy.'

Not all managers achieved the same high standard. The following spring, in April 2015, I was running the line in a Championship match between Brentford and Bolton Wanderers. Bolton had two stars leading their attack, Adam Le Fondre and the England and Liverpool legend, Emile Heskey. Le Fondre had scored over 250 goals in his career and was still very fast, but he didn't always time his runs right. In fact, I flagged him offside six times in the first half. That's a lot – certainly for one player. I was satisfied with each decision, but as we walked off at half time, I could see someone who wasn't: Neil Lennon, the Bolton manager, who was obviously very angry. When I was within five metres of him, he pointed directly at me and started shouting about the number of offsides I'd given, the implication being that I had it in for his team and was deliberately trying to sabotage their attack.

> ❝ Needless to say, the call never came.

I ignored him and kept walking towards our changing room. I certainly wasn't going to cave in to bullying. What mattered to me was what the assessor, David Phillips, thought. At the debrief after the match, he supported me – subject to the all-seeing DVD which he would study at his leisure. He called me the next day to confirm that each decision was correct and praised me for my accuracy. Nice one. 'I'm just waiting for a call from Neil Lennon to apologise for his rant,' I said. Needless to say, the call never came.

One last match stands out: Brighton and Hove Albion at home against Watford near the end of the season in April 2015. It was a big game – covered live by Sky – and Watford would almost certainly be promoted to the Premier League if they won. As a Luton supporter, that was the last thing I would have enjoyed, and before the kick-off I had the slightly spiteful pleasure of stamping on a few yellow balloons which had drifted down from the packed away stand. Keith Stroud, the referee, was also a Hatter, but I know we both worked hard to do our job without prejudice.

It was a good day – Brighton's Amex stadium is a warm and welcoming venue – and both teams played well. Keith also did his bit to keep his team's morale up by challenging us over the comms system during a break in play to think of a song with a colour in it – though not blue or yellow! That's the sort of thing no one knows about, but keeping both linos on the same page is part of the referee's job. We're physically far apart, but we have to work as a unit, and as I've mentioned before, when the team clicks it makes for a much better afternoon.

> ❝ I had the slightly spiteful pleasure of stamping on a few yellow balloons.

Both sides played fast, exciting football, and Watford came out 2-0 winners, which put them well on the path to Premiership glory. Among the very first people to congratulate their captain, Troy Deeney, were Keith and myself – life-long Luton supporters. But you couldn't begrudge them their success. Promotion from the Championship to the Premiership is one of the toughest things to achieve, and they had played well enough throughout the season to deserve it.

At the end of the afternoon, I sat in the changing room feeling absolutely shattered. I had had a good game – and indeed a good season – but was drained and ready to head home and enjoy a much-needed break. Had I done enough to achieve my season's ambition – promotion to the Select Group? I hoped so, but I had to wait for others to decide.

Before the 2015/16 season started, the PGMOL Conference saw the announcement of a Select Group 2 (SG2), which would come into operation in 2016/17. What it meant was that the top 30 assistant referees would be selected to officiate exclusively in the Championship. They would receive development coaching to qualify them for promotion to SG1 and the Premier League. The stakes were made higher by the fact that those not selected for SG2 would only be able to officiate in Leagues 1 and 2.

A new level in the hierarchy was being introduced. It could be the fast track to what everyone wanted: officiating in the Premier. But the downside was, if you didn't make it, you lost the Championship. It was a big deal for everyone. I knew I would be applying. Not to would simply be giving up – not only the dream of making it into the Premiership ranks, but relinquishing without a fight access to the highest standard below the Prem.

I was confident I was good enough and that my record would back that up. But my gnawing doubt was that the powers that be would prefer the SG2 list to be made up of people in their late twenties and early thirties. These were people likely to have a body fat percentage under 18. My best ever reading was 18.9%, three years before. In 2016, when SG2 started, I would be 46.

My selection stats weren't promising either. I had peaked in 2012/13 with 18 appointments to the Championship, and though the two following seasons had kept me in double figures, I felt I needed a big season to be a strong contender for the following year. And what happened? For the second time in my life, I fractured my elbow, this time tripping on a pavement as I went for a training run in January 2016. At least it was elbow singular rather than both, but even so I was off for over a month, losing valuable opportunities to impress those who would be making the crucial judgments when it came to SG2.

At home aged 5 and already on the ball.

World Cup final–Wembley, July 1966. L to r: Uwe Seeler, Tofiq Bahramov (linesman), Gottfried Dienst (referee), Karol Galba (linesman), Bobby Moore.
(Getty Images)

Wood End School, Harpenden – Football Team 1979-80 – aged 10, sitting at the right end of the front row.

In my Luton Town away shirt – 1983.

Team rivalry. Luton v Millwall – Kenilworth Road – March 1985 (Getty Images)

Heysel Disaster – May 1985.
(Getty Images)

An added bonus to winning the Under 15 Player of the Year Award at the 61FC awards evening at the Chiltern Hotel, Luton, was bumping into Gary Lineker. He happened to be checking in to meet up with the England squad who were on their way to Finland for a World Cup qualifier. I asked him to pose for a picture, and he agreed.
A nice man. May 1985.

The infamous "Hand of God".
Diego Maradona – Azteca Stadium, June 1986.
(Getty Images)

Kenilworth Road – referee for a friendly game on the plastic pitch, June 1987.

Hillsborough Disaster – April 1989.
(Getty Images)

Subsequently I go to Anfield and see the Hillsborough tributes, and I also laid down some flowers and a Luton scarf, 22 April 1989.

Malmö, Sweden – Euro 92 Tournament – June 1992. Note the incorrect wording on the poster behind me which includes Yugoslavia who had been expelled from the tournament when the Balkan War started and replaced by Denmark – who, in turn, then went on to win it.

With my fellow England fans – Poland v England – Katowice – May 1993.

That goal! Paul Gascoigne at his finest. England v Scotland – Wembley, June 1996...
(Getty Images)

... and I was there. I record the Wembley scoreboard – England v Scotland, June 1996.

The "Ghost Goal". Luiz Garcia – Anfield, May 2005.
(Getty Images)

L to r: Mike George (assistant referee), Paul Taylor (referee), and me (assistant referee) waiting for the pitch to be cleared so we can carry on with the game
– Upton Park, August 2009.
(Getty Images)

Another "Ghost Goal".
Frank Lampard
– England v Germany,
June 2010.
(Getty Images)

The 4th Official must
keep a cool head under all
circumstances
– Stevenage v Bradford City,
August 2013.
(Kevin Coleman)

The perfect flag position!
Northampton Town v Scunthorpe
United, January 2017.
(Peter Norton)

Dreaming of a bright future for
Luton Town! Within touching
distance of the UEFA Champions
League Trophy and the UEFA Europa
League Trophy, October 2019.

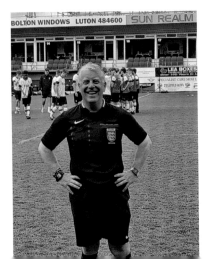

Kenilworth Road – referee for a
U18 trial game, May 2021.

Along with 50 or so others, I was invited to Assessment Day in April. I knew I had a chance. I had been a specialist assistant referee since 2012, and on the National List since 2008. I had been trusted with some big games and was certainly experienced enough. I could only do my best and hope. But of course, everyone else who turned up on the day at Warwick University was making the same commitment.

It wasn't *The Hunger Games* or the matinee at the Colosseum. We all knew each other through working together and certainly didn't wish anyone ill. All the same, the numbers were unavoidable: 30 places with 50-plus people competing for them. It was tough. We were tested on our knowledge of the Laws of the Game; then there was analysis of match day incidents. There was even a mock-TV interview to test mental strength and resilience under hostile questioning. I was pretty confident I had done well on that side of things.

On the physical side, I just ran until I collapsed.

But it wasn't enough. The email came a fortnight later, and to say I was gutted would be an understatement. I was more than disappointed. I felt rejected and angry. I thought I had done well enough and could still do well officiating in the Championship. I had been happy mixing Championship matches with League 1 and 2 matches. But in the all-or-nothing world of the new dispensation, that was no longer possible, and I was left with – well, not nothing, because I was still in the Football League and had had some wonderful experiences with the lower clubs over the years. But I was worried that it wouldn't feel the same as when I knew I'd have a bigger match to look forward to in a week or so. Without that, would there be enough to keep me going?

To make matters worse, the following evening I was at AFC Wimbledon v Portsmouth, and the three other match officials had all made it to SG2. They assumed I had been too and congratulated me on going up a notch with them. The collective mood changed when I told them that I wouldn't be joining them. They were sympathetic, but I was feeling tender about it, so it felt as though they were pitying me – which I hated.

But we were there to take care of a match, so we were soon in our positions doing our jobs. But although the game went well, I drove home feeling upset and wondering about my future. My last game of the season was a couple of weeks later. I didn't want it to be my last game, full stop. I was not ready to quit. I still wanted to be on the National List and to try again for SG2. I vowed to train hard over the summer and give it another crack.

97

On the face of it, preparations for the 2016/17 were exactly the same as they had been for the last few years. I attended the PGMOL conference and collected my kit and kit bag, and then the following month went to Nuneaton for the fitness test. I had promised myself I would put my all into it, and I did. With a trackside temperature of 34°C, I needed real determination and a very positive attitude to get through my ten laps. I was drained afterwards, but passed, as I always had in previous years.

The big difference was the prospect of a season without Championship football. I got a strong taste of what that was going to be like when my appointment for the first day of the season was as fourth official for Portsmouth v Carlisle United. Everyone hopes to be officiating at a game on the opening day, and someone has to do the chores with the numbers board and take the chat from the technical area. But on that occasion, I really didn't want that person to be me.

I got more action in my next few matches – at Leyton Orient, Barnet, AFC Wimbledon, Oxford United and Southend. It wasn't that I minded League 1 and League 2 games. Each game was enjoyable. It's just that each game was also at the same level as the previous one.

Maybe that made me a bit flat. I certainly had a shock at a game at the end of August. It was a Football League U23 Trophy match between Charlton Athletic and Southampton. It was a competitive encounter, which Charlton won on penalties. I thought I'd had a good game. There were no controversial decisions, and I was feeling upbeat when the four officials gathered for the debrief. But a single remark by the assessor, Kelvin Morton, was devastating. He said that, in his opinion, I wasn't fit enough to run the line, as I wasn't keeping up with the players. Before I could respond to that, he observed that, as I had passed the fitness test, I must be fit enough so therefore wasn't trying hard enough.

I was gobsmacked. It's never a good idea to argue with an assessor, so I kept quiet. But the comments stung. This was the first time my fitness had been called into question. The one year I had failed the pre-season fitness test, I had passed the retake. I had never given less than 100% and certainly hadn't been slacking. The thing Kelvin seemed to be overlooking was that the players were all 25 years younger than me and training full-time. Of course they were faster than me. I felt I had kept up with the play and there were no criticisms of my decisions. It was another blow to my confidence, another punch on the bruise I'd already sustained. If people were now doubting me, maybe my time at the top was running out.

In September 2016, I refereed the Beds FA Premier Cup final between Barton Rovers and Luton Town. I really enjoyed it and started thinking about returning to refereeing. Back on the line in the League games, I tried my hardest every time and still got satisfaction from being involved, especially at Portsmouth, Millwall and Peterborough. There was an interesting match in October 2016 when Charlton Athletic hosted Coventry City, and both sets of fans staged a protest against their clubs' owners. The match was halted for five minutes immediately after kick-off when hundreds of toy pigs were thrown onto the pitch.

But despite these good days, I felt my enthusiasm was beginning to wane. I'd always believed that I was one of the most committed officials on the list, but if that was no longer the case, then I realised I had some serious thinking to do.

Around Christmas, the PGMOL proposed a change to the pre-season fitness procedure. It would now include the dreaded CODA (Change of Direction Analysis) test. This involved a mixture of sidestepping, turning and sprinting over a distance of 10m. I had done this before at the SG2 assessment day and knew that completing it under the required 10 seconds was going to be hard. I practised it in a few sessions at home and was always about a second or two over. Not good enough.

I had seen people fail the summer fitness test and end their careers there and then on the track. Imagine that – the whole new season just stripped from you a month before it started. That wasn't for me. I wanted to know my last game was going to be my last game so I could savour it. I wanted to end my time on the National List on my own terms – not embarrassing myself by failing the fitness test and suffering the knowing looks of the PGMOL sports scientists as they recorded my results on their clipboards.

When it came down to it, the choice wasn't hard. I would retire – on my own terms. I gave myself Christmas to discuss it at home and see that the decision sat comfortably with me. And then I wrote to Dave Allison early in the New Year saying I was resigning from the National List of Assistant Referees at the end of the season. My plan was to return to being a Level 3 referee for the FA. I read it over a couple of times before I pressed 'Send' because I knew that there would be no going back. Once it had gone – beyond recall – I felt a big sense of relief. I was owning my destiny, and that felt good.

Dave replied to say he was surprised by my decision but that he respected it. So that was that. I had four months left.

I enjoyed my last matches, travelling to clubs like Notts County, Cheltenham, Northampton Town and Cambridge United for reasonably matched encounters between reasonably skilled full-time professional footballers – some on the way up and some on the way down (like me). I had a couple more run-ins with my assessors. Kelvin Morton (again) criticised me for taking too long to get ready when I had to replace an injured assistant at Charlton in February 2017. I had trouble resetting my communication system as well as taking my tracksuit off and putting on the right colour shirt. I tried to do it as quickly as possible, but hurrying it was only going to make it more likely that I prolonged the hold-up. Once again, I held my tongue, but did phone Dave Allison on the Monday to give him my side of the story.

At Gillingham, I was praised on the day for signalling a penalty, but then a few days later, after the DVD review showed I'd got it marginally wrong, my assessment was adjusted down to 'developmental advice'. With the end of the season – and my PGMOL career – in sight, it was a bit late for that.

In April 2017, I was running the line at Northampton Town v Sheffield United. It was a hot sunny spring afternoon, and Sheffield United won to secure promotion. Their supporters invaded the pitch three times, but with no malice intended: they were just expressing their delight at their team's success. As senior assistant, I was near the technical area, and in one of the pitch invasions some joker in fancy dress went up to the Northampton manager, Justin Edinburgh, and gestured rudely in his face. Justin just stared at him until he cleared off. When I next had the chance, I checked Justin was OK. He said he was fine. I smiled and said, 'I know who I'd have backed in a fight!' He smiled back. A decent man. Sadly, he passed away two years later from a cardiac arrest at the young age of 49.

May 2017 saw my last match as a National List assistant referee, a League 2 encounter between Crewe Alexandra and Barnet. One last new ground to experience and a lively game, with the hosts winning comfortably 4-1. It was an enjoyable occasion, with enough to do to keep my thoughts off the final whistle and what it would signify for me. When the referee, John Brooks, looked at his watch and blew that final whistle, I felt numb... That was it. All over.

There wasn't much time to take in the atmosphere for the last time. The home supporters were sprinting jubilantly onto the pitch to celebrate the end of the season, and I had to move swiftly towards the tunnel. As I darted off the field of play, I snatched a last look back as a National List assistant.

Back in the changing room, John produced a bottle of champagne courtesy of the Football League, and the assessor, Uriah Rennie, said some nice words as well. I'm not sure he bothered with an actual assessment, but

I was satisfied with my last performance and happy to go out with pats on the back, a bottle of bubbly and my head held high. I was sad it was over but grateful for the nine seasons I'd spent on the List.

I'd decided to do the trip by train. Given the awkward drive and the excellent rail service to Crewe, it was the sensible option. But it meant I missed the privacy of the car where I could review the day and think quietly about the future. As I looked around Crewe station that Saturday evening, I suddenly had to face the fact that I was now outside the PGMOL bubble – forever. I realised that no one knew who I was, no one knew why I was there. And no one cared.

Time to move on.

In June 2017, the PGMOL gave me and all that season's other retirees a leaving banquet, and at the PGMOL conference I was presented with a certificate of service for my nine seasons on the National List.

That August, I returned to officiating as a Level 3 referee in the Southern League – Aylesbury United v Beaconsfield Town was my first match. I was back where I'd come from some 16 years earlier. As they say, what goes up must come down.

CHAPTER CHALLENGE ANSWERS

1. *Award a free kick for the foul as no other offence has been committed yet.*

2. *Yes – you cannot be in an offside position in your own half, but you can commit an offside offence in your own half. This happens if you get involved in active play in your own half, having gone back into your own half from an offside position in the opponent's half.*

CHAPTER 11

The Best Party

Reflections on a Career

When I ended my time on the National List of Assistant Referees, I was pleased with my exit, glad I had taken control of the process. I'd given the PGMOL four months' notice, so I would get my wish of knowing that my last game was my last game and could savour the final matches as I counted down to the end of my time as an AR at nearly the highest level possible. I was also pleased that the FA were happy to take me back as a Level 3 referee for the following season, so I would continue my career as a match official.

The send-off was also pleasing. I attended the leavers' event in June 2017 accompanied by Jacqueline, and at my last PGMOL conference I was given my certificate of service. All of this was as I planned it. I had wanted to leave through the 'front door' with good wishes rather than be forced to retire early through injury or a failed fitness test. I'd seen colleagues go that way, and each time it was a personal tragedy. I just knew that it was the right time to leave, and that knowledge made the wrench to end my PGMOL career more bearable.

My life on the line as an assistant referee on the National List felt like a winning lottery ticket. I hope I've conveyed something of the excitement I felt. Match day was always the week's highlight. Walking through the 'Players and Officials' entrance at the stadium wearing my PGMOL suit and tie never failed to make me feel great. Officials were always treated like VIPs, which was good for our self-esteem. Imposter syndrome maybe?

But I certainly didn't feel an imposter as a match official. A passionate

CHAPTER CHALLENGES

1. Two players slide off the pitch in wet conditions. The ball remains in play and one player grabs the other player's leg to stop them getting to the ball first. What do you do?

2. What shape can the goalposts and crossbar be?

football fan first and foremost, I knew that the game is about the players and the supporters. No one pays money to watch the referee and assistant referees. If we could keep a low profile, that was exactly how we liked it.

If none of the spectators could remember anything any of us did during the course of the match, that was perfect! But I felt proud to be part of the team that made the occasion work for everyone present.

> ❝ I know the game is about players and supporters.

It's already been five years since I left the PGMOL and the National List of Assistant Referees and, of course, there are some things I miss more than others: the thrill of walking down the tunnel at 2.55pm to be greeted by the roar of the crowd; working well in a team with colleagues; the unscripted moments when players or managers react well to you, and the flashes of humour that of course the wider public aren't party to. I also miss the money that we got paid each month. This didn't amount to much, but it averaged around £8,000 per year by the end, which is a pretty good reward for doing something you absolutely love!

Overall, I spent 22 seasons from 1995 to 2017 taking refereeing very seriously. Looking back, I know that I made every effort to make the most of my ability. I feel that I got as high as I could, though that didn't stop me dreaming. Of course, I'd have loved to have risen to the Premier League, and how special would it have been to officiate at Wembley? But it was not to be.

When football was my priority, I know I missed out on other things. My son and daughter are both now in their mid-twenties, but I was away for a high proportion of family time when they were growing up, leaving my ex-wife Ruth holding the fort Saturday after Saturday (plus weekdays when I was officiating). I missed parents' evenings, birthday celebrations, social events, school sports days and quality time with friends and family, especially over Christmas, Easter and during the summer holidays.

When I met Jacqueline in 2007, one of the first things I told her was that I was seriously into football and that this would impact her. Not only would I be the Invisible Man most Saturdays, but professional football takes up most of the year. The season ends in May, but pre-season starts in July, leaving only June for holidays. Not a bad time of the year, but it's a small window.

In addition to the time taken up being a match official, I had to maintain the high fitness levels required. This took up four evenings a week, and I often didn't get home before 8 o'clock in the evening. Getting the balance right between the time refereeing takes up (training/matches/conferences/meetings/workshops, etc.), time at work and then spending time with family is hard to get right. Sometimes I managed it and sometimes I didn't.

I was made redundant in January 2012, moving from Teaching Personnel to working freelance as a business trainer. This allowed me to manage my own diary and be available for refereeing whenever I wanted. It also meant I didn't have to ask for time off when I needed to get away, which had always made me feel a bit guilty.

Since becoming freelance, I've managed to keep earning enough to support the living standard I've been accustomed to. But things have improved for officials since I retired, and now the compensation is enough to allow for a full-time commitment, especially at Premiership level. This ensures a full time and professional focus on training, diet, fitness and professional development.

> Sometimes I managed it and sometimes I didn't.

According to nationalworld.com and givemesport.com, the salaries available for Premier League officials are as follows:

Referees – retainer worth £38,500 to £42,000 and then approx. £1,500 per match

Assistant referees – retainer worth £30,000 and then approx. £850 per match

Video assistant referees - retainer worth £30,000 and then approx. £850 per match

Of course, the above can't compare to the salaries paid to the players, but compared to the wages of the average supporter, it's a generous remuneration for doing something you feel privileged to be doing.

When I look back at my nine seasons on the National List of Assistant Referees, I feel immensely grateful for the experience I had. I worked hard and put in a lot of effort. I made sacrifices regarding other parts of my life and missed some important things, but overall, the joy of being involved with the best game in the world was irresistible. If I had my time again, would I do it all again? Of course I would – with no hesitation at all.

Each year, people leave the National List and new people join. When I joined in 2008, Steve Tincknell was one of those who was leaving, and he took a moment to share an insight with me. He said, with genuine feeling, 'It's the best party you'll ever be invited to!'

He was right. It was.

CHAPTER CHALLENGES ANSWERS

1. *Award a direct free kick against the offending player to be taken at the nearest boundary line to where the offence occurred.*

2. *Round, square or elliptical.*

PART 4

THE UNOFFICIAL GUIDE
TO LIFE AS A
FOOTBALL OFFICIAL

CHAPTER 12

1863 and All That

The Laws of the Game and How We Got them

The origins of football go back into the mists of time, with theories as to which culture thought of it first ranging from the use of heads for a kick-about after yet another victory for Genghis Khan's Mongolian armies, to a rather more effete prodding of a soft ball about a palace in France. Even the Pilgrim Fathers arrived in America to find the Native Indians talking of *Pasukkquakkohowog*, loosely translated as 'gathering to play football'. But as with so many sports, Britain likes to pride itself on being the home of 'the beautiful game'. Certainly, the historic record extends back down the centuries – mainly through accounts of the authorities trying to stamp it out and punish those who played it. Shakespeare references the game in *King Lear*, with one character denigrating another as a 'base football player' while neatly tripping him up. Football has always been associated with physical aggression, often escalating into violence. Research suggests that in the 16th century, more people died playing football than taking part in any other recreational activity, apart from archery.

CHAPTER CHALLENGES

1. *A defender takes a free kick and passes it back to his goalie... who misses the ball, and it rolls into the goal. What do you do?*

2. *What happens if the ball accidentally hits the referee during play?*

In its earliest manifestation, football was played by mobs of men representing their communities in fierce local rivalries: village against village, or one end of town against the other. It was a rough-and-ready activity with few rules, traditionally played to celebrate religious holidays. The aim was to get the 'ball' – an inflated pig's bladder or bundle of rags sewn up in a sack – into one goal or the other over distances which could extend more than a mile. The Shrovetide football match in Ashbourne, Derbyshire, can be dated back to 1667 but boasts medieval roots.

The village divides into Up'ards and Down'ards and the goals are three miles apart.

In some cases, teams had to get the ball into their own goal, but the challenge was the same: to win the contest for territorial domination using whatever physical force was necessary. Football demonstrated the truth of George Orwell's observation that sport is 'war without the shooting'. Matches were basically battles, rumbling brawls of sweating and swearing combatants. Each location had its unique features, spawning varying tactics. In the town of Derby – the origin of the 'derby' match between local rivals – the game or battle often ended up with the ball in the river, where players readily risked drowning to wrest it from their opponents.

Onlookers could hardly distinguish the difference between the game and a riot, and just as bear-baiting and public executions began to be questioned as wholesome family entertainment, the prejudice against ferocious street fighting hardened. On many occasions, the Riot Act was actually read and the local military summoned. But the hunger for afternoons of gleeful savagery was not easily suppressed, and the medieval mayhem persisted.

In the parallel universe of the public schools (the exclusive preserve of the sons of the aristocratic and affluent), gleeful savagery was also popular. For generations, the boys were left largely to their own devices outside the classroom, and in most schools the pupils governed their own recreations. If the masters took any interest, it was mainly hostile. One public school cricket team insisted on playing a match against their rivals, despite their headmaster's prohibition. He flogged every member of the eleven when they returned from the match – even though they had triumphed.

The Duke of Wellington claimed the Battle of Waterloo was won on the playing fields of Eton. The brutality of the sports they played prepared his young officers for the extraordinary violence of close-range combat, in which the unprotected infantry had to withstand repeated cavalry charges and volleys of close-range artillery fire (hence the expression 'cannon fodder').

But in the peace that Waterloo guaranteed, England softened slightly, and with the young Queen Victoria on the throne, the country began a radical transformation. As the new tidal wave of piety swept through society, it revolutionised education and changed views on sport. Dr Arnold, the reforming headmaster of Rugby School, was a scholar and committed Christian. He was concerned with the spiritual wellbeing of his pupils and could see the benefit of games: organised exercise would be a healthy distraction from youthful temptations. The idea of 'muscular Christianity' caught on, and it wasn't long before cohorts of pupils were actively encouraged to run out onto muddy pitches to kick each other merrily till the bell rang for evening prayers in the school chapel.

Cricket or rowing took up the summer term, but football dominated the long months of autumn and winter. War without the shooting took pride of place at all the great public schools. But each had its own version of the game. As an Etonian, George Orwell would have witnessed – and possibly even taken part in – the famous Eton Wall Game, which set two teams fighting their way up and down the wall in question in an effort to score a goal through one of the two tiny apertures available at either end. This achievement was a rarity, and with a strike rate of three goals per century, it is not surprising that the Wall Game did not spread beyond the bounds of the College.

❝ War without the shooting.

The Wall Game was not Eton's only contribution to sporting history. Less well known is the Eton Field Game, which, as its name suggests, used a field instead of a wall as the territory to be fought over. And for some historians, this was the template for modern football, though many other schools could make a similar claim.

Each institution had its own form of the game, peculiar to its own traditions and circumstances. City schools didn't have playing fields, so made do with courts and cloisters. There were no commonly agreed rules, so instead of playing their local rivals, schools played their own versions of football among their own pupils, enhancing the intensity of competition by offering cups and house colours to successful teams. Each version was clearly a variation of the same game: all were territorial, with goals the object. In most, the ball could be thrown, but the catcher could only kick it. And kicking wasn't limited to the ball. 'Hacking' was part and parcel of the sport, along with barging and scragging (but not actual punching).

There were various rules for what happened when the ball ended up over the by-line. The one thing you couldn't do was pass the ball forwards. The offside rule was that basically everybody was offside all the time, so if you wanted to score a goal, you

❝ Hacking was part and parcel of the sport.

either had to form a brutal wedge of a scrum and force your way through to your opponents' goal or break away and dribble the ball to within shooting distance before the defending mob dragged you down like a pack of hounds. When a pupil at Rugby put the ball under his arm and sprinted for the line, he was sewing the seed of an eventual schism between rugby and football, but for the time being it was regarded as simply an exuberant misuse of initiative.

Unlike cricket, whose Laws had been established by the MCC in the 18th century, football had no governing or rule-giving body, so there was no method by which the rules of the game could be consolidated. That became a problem for public school boys when they moved on to their universities and wanted to play football against students from other schools. Many formed Old Boys' teams and regularly returned to their own schools to play their successors.

But more adventurous souls at Cambridge decided to tackle the problem head-on and called a meeting to see if a general set of rules – or laws – couldn't be agreed. In 1848, there was a meeting to which representatives of all the great footballing schools were invited. The hope was to produce a set of Cambridge Rules accepted by all.

It took more than one meeting to agree on such basics as whether hacking should continue to be allowed. For some, a game that didn't allow you to kick an opponent was simply a waste of time. Then there was the question of carrying the ball. Many traditions allowed for the ball to be caught and then kicked; but clearly running with it was beyond the pale.

The Cambridge meetings failed. But they were not forgotten. Football would continue in its disparate paths for a few more years. Eventually, in November 1863, a meeting was called in a Lincoln's Inn Fields tavern attended by representatives of eleven Old Boys' clubs to thrash out a definitive version of the rules. The two main bones of contention were still catching and running versus kicking and dribbling, and the old debate over hacking. This self-selected group formed the Football Association (FA) and finally confirmed the unbridgeable chasm between football and rugby, while toning down the acceptable level of physical aggression.

The first edition of the FA's rules still looks pretty weird to the modern eye. There was no touchline for a start (so no linesmen). But there were two referees, who adjudicated on the ball going out of play. In an entirely amateur world, players were trusted to monitor such things scrupulously. The captains took responsibility for their players' behaviour, but in the unlikely event of a final decision being required, there was an all-powerful umpire. You could still catch the ball but had to kick it if you did so. There was no such thing as a corner – or a crossbar. The two uprights set eight yards apart were flimsier than they are today, with just a light rope tied between them, presumably at the height of the two tallest players taking part in the match.

The evolution of the offside rule could fill several sizeable tomes (we give it more attention later on), but it was at this stage so draconian that passing was virtually impossible. Which left attacking options limited to the traditional juggernaut of a scrum or the individual brilliance of a talented dribbler. If the goalkeeper got in your way, you were perfectly entitled to bowl him over. With a formation of seven or eight forwards, one or two defenders and a goalkeeper, the Victorian game still had more in common with 'mob' football than 'the beautiful game' followed by countless millions today. Oh, and every time a goal was scored, the two teams changed ends.

These Laws were under constant review and, with the majority of teams agreeing to play under them, they were gradually honed into the workable code that extended throughout the United Kingdom and thence to the rest of the world.

But it would be wrong to suggest that football as we know it owes everything to a bunch of top-hatted ex-public school toffs. For the alternative narrative, we must travel to the north and where the working-class game came into its own.

As we have seen the chaotic flood of 'folk' or mob football battles had been choked off by the prim Victorians, but though damned from the pulpit and the magistrates' bench, football could no more be dammed than a real river. The southern public schoolboys may have established a national organisation and made a first stab at a consistent code for the game, but there were other football centres in the north of the country, the most prominent being Sheffield, whose first football club (which was not related to its successors, Sheffield Wednesday and Sheffield United) was formed in 1857 by a group of local industrialists. Its original membership was middle class – largely the sons of chairmen and managers of the steel trade. Many were educated at the Sheffield Collegiate School, though the importance of the great southern public schools was acknowledged when the club's first secretary wrote to them all requesting copies of their rules before amalgamating them into a workable version for the north.

This was first published in 1858, five years before the FA's first attempt. It was by no means perfect. An obvious flaw was limiting the width of the goal to four yards. This inevitably resulted in far too many goalless draws, even though there was no offside rule. But the fact that there was a code and that other clubs in South Yorkshire were prepared to play according to it meant that the game expanded rapidly, and crowds increased exponentially. The rules established a veneer of order, but the visceral aggression of the old folk version of the game remained just below the surface. In 1862, in a match between Sheffield and rivals Hallam, a personal vendetta between two players triggered a wholesale battle between the sides and their supporters at Bramwell Lane Cricket Club.

The game also began to widen its base, with working men being granted time off work to play. Standards improved; matches were arranged across the Pennines as Lancashire teams drawing on mill workers sprang up, and the game also extended to Nottinghamshire, and then Birmingham with the foundation of Aston Villa in 1874.

There was a clear danger of the country simply splitting into two footballing tribes, one southern, posh and privileged; the other northern and predominantly working class. The Football Association probably would not have survived without the loyalty of the hugely influential Sheffield Club. In addition to the Laws of the Game that the FA published and revised through the 1860s, the founding of the FA Cup in 1871 established the country's first nationwide competition.

The early years of the Cup were dominated by public school and university teams, most notably the Old Etonians. Surprisingly, in 1879, a small Lancashire mill side, Darwen, travelled all the way to London to hold the Etonians, captained by the charismatic Arthur Kinnaird, chairman of the FA, to a draw, after being 5-1 down at half time.

The man who made the difference was Fergie Suter, who with his close friend Jimmy Love had been lured down to Lancashire from Glasgow with promises of employment and under-the-desk payments. Whether it was this travesty of the amateur code that made Kinnaird refuse the visitors the chance to settle the quarter-final in extra time isn't known, but the Darwen team had to make the long journey home and be prepared to be back at work in their mills first thing on Monday morning and then do it all again in a replay. The replay also ended in a draw (2-2) and the tie was only settled, once more down south, when the Etonians finally triumphed over their gutsy but exhausted working-class opponents 6-2.

> " Early years of the Cup were dominated by public schools and university teams.

Suter's story, entertainingly told in the recent Netflix miniseries, *The English Game*, is the perfect illustration of football's inevitable swing towards working-class domination. Suter, determined to achieve FA Cup success, was soon tempted to change allegiance, moving from Darwen to Blackburn the following season. The town had two teams, Blackburn Olympic and Blackburn Rovers. Suter joined Rovers, reaching the FA Cup final against the

Old Etonians in 1882 at its recently adopted home, the Oval cricket ground. Once again, Kinnaird led his Old Boys to victory by the single goal of the match. That was the last time a team representing the social elite lifted the cup after dominating the first ten years of the competition. The following year, Blackburn Olympic finally banished Kinnaird's all-conquering veterans to become the first working-class team to win the FA Cup. In 1884, Suter's Blackburn Rovers finally won, defeating the Scottish champions Queen's Park 2-1 in front of at least 10,000 spectators.

It's a measure of the strength of Scottish football that, on the same day, the Scottish national team, which would usually have featured several Queen's Park players, were playing Wales, whom they beat easily. In fact, Scotland's role in developing the modern game was out of all proportion to its population. Glasgow was the epicentre, with two giant football clubs, Rangers and Celtic, achieving the prominence and outreach way beyond anything south of the border. While many English clubs still played on cricket grounds – the FA Cup remained at the Oval for many years – both Glasgow clubs soon had stadiums capable of hosting crowds in excess of 20,000 spectators. By the turn of the century, after extensive redevelopment, both Ibrox and Celtic Park could easily host over 60,000.

What sucked such vast numbers through the turnstiles was the quality of the football on offer. Suter and Jimmy Love had astonished their English teammates with the finesse of their passing game. But this was commonplace in Scotland, where the sport had never had to disentangle itself from the handling game. While the Old Etonians were still trundling up and down in their scrum formation, Scottish players were developing a far higher skillset and an infinitely more sophisticated strategy.

But there was more than connoisseurship involved. Old Firm matches between Celtic and Rangers were driven by the fiercest of all British football rivalries inflamed by sectarian affiliations. The result was a level of violence and destruction unknown in the English game, resulting in regular pitch invasions, fights between fans and assaults on referees. The level of disorder shook the middle classes and drew the condemnation of the press. One journalist tagged an episode as 'worthy of a band of drunken cannibals', although no evidence of actual flesh-eating was cited. The ratcheting violence culminated in the world's first football stadium disaster when in 1902 seething crowds caused sufficient mayhem for lives to be lost in the collapsed West Tribune Stand at Ibrox during a game between Scotland and England.

Whether the dangers of playing in their native land had any bearing on their career decisions or not, a great many Scottish footballers followed

Suter and Jimmy Love to pastures new south of the border. By the late 1880s, the Championship teams of Preston North End and Sunderland in the 1890s were made up largely of Scottish stars.

By the turn of the century, most of the components of the modern game were in place. Leagues with their various divisions had been established; clubs had their own grounds with terraces and grandstands for spectators; and after several years of anguished debate, the FA capitulated over the question of amateurism. This was under the leadership of Arthur Kinnaird, who saw that the Football Association would be left behind if it refused to accept economic reality and drop the ban on professionalism. Despite his old school affiliations – he played in his long trousers and maintained his brutal physicality throughout his playing days – Kinnaird had the game's best interests at heart and remained Chairman of the FA for 30 years, ensuring that the elite retained its power to influence future developments, even as the game solidified into the nation's working-class sport.

The FA's main role was organising the ever-expanding league system, arranging the fixture list and organising the Cup. To boost its authority, in 1892 the FA invited the Prince of Wales to become its patron. He continued in the role when he became King on the death of his mother in 1901. And when he died in 1910, his son, George V, continued the association. The royal connection continues to this day.

The FA also retained control of the Laws of the Game. After the seismic parting of the ways between football and rugby, the rest of the regulations regarding pitch markings, wooden crossbars, nets in the goals, etc. fell into place with each revision. In 1871, the specific position of the goalkeeper was acknowledged, with strict rules covering what was allowed and what was not. Four years later, teams stopped changing ends after each goal, leaving it to half time. And in 1877, the throw-in (or 'throw-*on*') was allowed to go in any direction, rather than just at right-angles from the touchline.

Where, I hear you ask, was the linesman, marking the point at which the ball crossed the line? Some way off in the future, is the answer. That was because matches were still controlled by two umpires, overseen by a referee. In many instances, the umpires were the team captains who were pledged to maintain fair play as a matter of honour. (The Corinthians, the cream of the amateur cream, regarded penalties as morally beneath them. If awarded one, a player would disdainfully kick it wide.)

But with the irreversible expansion of professionalism, it became clear there needed to be a change to reflect the changes in the game. In 1891, the referee moved onto the field of play and the two umpires – no long team captains – were sent to run the line with sticks! These could be raised not only to indicate where the ball had crossed the line but to allow an appeal for a foul from either captain. In due course, it was realised that flags would be more immediately visible.

As time went on, referees gradually increased their power over the game, relegating the umpires to subsidiary duties. But astonishingly, the actual role of the linesman was not introduced – under Law 6 – until 1938.

The linesman's flag had an interesting evolution from the stick of the early days to the sophisticated piece of technology that we know today. To begin with, the two linesmen were distinguished by flags of different colours to denote seniority. And that was important because, before the fourth official, the higher-ranked linesman had to run the line in front of the dugout, dealing with coaches and managers and overseeing substitutions when they entered the game. He would also be the one to take over duties if the referee was injured.

The flag has always been the focus of attention, and at some stage during the Second World War, someone had the bright idea of giving them lights. That might seem strange, but the big cities were still beset with terrible smogs which could plunge any winter afternoon into stygian gloom. Besides, throughout the hostilities, there were an awful lot of boffins inventing weird and wonderful ways of defeating the enemy. It just needed one football-mad engineer with the run of an Army workshop and a bit of free time, and there you have it: the luminous lino's flag!

A historical instance of its use came in November 1945 when Moscow's Dynamo team came on a celebratory tour of the UK, playing one match in Scotland and three in England. They played Arsenal, albeit on Tottenham's pitch, and were treated to a London peasouper, which reduced visibility to virtually nothing. Which in turn reduced the proceedings to the level of farce. The Russians had brought their own referee, who did things the Russian way, and the two English linesmen ended up on the same touchline, peering hopelessly through the faint halos of light given off by their flags. The match ended in victory for the visitors 4-3, but no two accounts of it would be the same.

In 1947 yellow flags were introduced (with no requirement to light up), and in 1956 IFAB introduced red and yellow flags for international matches. The flag's evolution continued to become the highly technological bit of kit it is today. Flags now have a buzzer button that sends a signal to the receiver pack worn on the upper arm to attract the referee's attention. This great but unseen advance has dramatically improved communication between the match officials. And better communications = better decisions = better games.

In Law, signals from the assistants are merely advisory and only the referee has the power to award anything, from throw-ins to penalties. But of course, in the modern game, officiating is based on good communications and teamwork.

(PS See Appendix for further flag information, including cost!)

CHAPTER CHALLENGES ANSWERS

1. *Award a corner kick – Law says you cannot score an own goal from a free kick.*

2. *The ball is deemed out of play if the ball remains on the field, but a team then starts an attack, or the ball directly goes into the goal or the team in possession of the ball changes. Play is stopped and restarted with a dropped ball.*

CHAPTER 13

So You Want to be a Referee's Assistant?

A Few Insights

I've already told you how I became a referee's assistant. A love of the game, recognition that I wasn't going to be good enough to play football professionally, but an equally strong realisation that I wanted to remain involved brought me to the inevitable conclusion that I should be a match official. One way or the other, it'll be the same for pretty much every referee and AR around the world. In some places, it is easier than in others – especially for women.

It is incredible to think that in living memory, some keen football participants were banned. For being female.

In 1971, Léa Campos was a qualified referee in Brazil but the CBD, Brazil's sporting authority, refused her permission to officiate. In charge of the CBD was João Havelange, who went on to be president of FIFA. Havelange apparently told Campos that *'women's bodies weren't suitable for refereeing men's games'* and also that *'having periods would make things difficult'*.

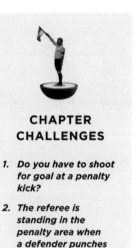

CHAPTER CHALLENGES

1. **Do you have to shoot for goal at a penalty kick?**

2. **The referee is standing in the penalty area when a defender punches them in the face. The offender is shown a red card – how is the match restarted?**

Refusing to be defeated, Campos campaigned for a change in Brazil's sporting laws. The authorities had refused to give her a licence, claiming the legislation that banned female footballers in Brazil also banned female officials. Campos spent years fighting with the CBD and Havelange and tried to promote her cause by refereeing in friendly matches between women players that were often broken up by police.

In 1971, Campos begged a local commander to help her secure an audience with President Médici and was granted three minutes. They met at the presidential palace in Brasilia. Medici supported Campos and her ambitions and overruled Havelange. In July that year, after a 'change of heart', Campos was allowed to officiate as a referee.

Campos officiated in 98 lower division matches in Brazil and her presence was promoted as an exotic attraction. Newspapers carried articles suggesting that the players would be aroused by a female referee.

Alas, a bad traffic accident brought her career to a premature end. She has since married and moved to live in the USA.

Her battle for equality and her legacy is secured in history forever.

In England, the career path is carefully mapped out. At the start, when you officiate in local football, you are registered with the County FA where you live. As you progress through the ranks (depending on performance), you automatically become registered with the FA in London as well, and they can appoint you to games in certain leagues and cup competitions under their jurisdiction. You can also join the Referees Association (RA), which is an organisation involved in mentoring, welfare, training and development.

When you get high enough up the ladder to be promoted to the National List as a referee or an assistant referee, you also automatically become part of the PGMOL (Professional Game Match Officials Ltd), the organisation responsible for the match officials who operated in the Premier League and three divisions of the English Football League (EFL). The PGMOL also appoint you to matches in the professional competitions.

> **The FA didn't openly support Poll.**

The PGMOL was formed in 2001, when referees in England became professional, and it is funded by the FA, the Premier League and the EFL. Its role is to enforce the Law for its stakeholders, which should place its members above the fray. But in a dispute between an official and a club, it often turns out that the individual is outranked by the club. An example of this is the row between John Terry of Chelsea and referee Graham Poll in November 2006. Terry was England captain and was sent off by Poll when playing in a game for Chelsea at Tottenham. Chelsea disputed the reasons for the sending-off and the FA didn't openly support Poll.

Talking of ranks, there is a three-tier system in the PGMOL: Select Group 1 – SG1 – officiate in the Premier League; Select Group 2 – SG2 – officiate in the Championship; and those in the National List – NL – officiate in Leagues 1 and 2.

Advancement from NL to SG2 and then SG1 is by invitation, subject to marks awarded for performance. These marks are used to create the Merit List, which is similar to a league table. Those at the top of the Merit List are considered for promotion at the end of each season. Those at the bottom may find themselves demoted. This really matters, as those in SG1 are full-time officials. It is their job and paid accordingly. No one wants to lose their place at the top table. As an added incentive, there is a performance-related bonus paid according to each official's position on the Merit List. The higher up the List you go, the more money you get. Does this produce better performances? You can be the judge of that.

In England at any one time, there are approximately 30,000 qualified referees. In the PGMOL, there are about 300 match officials. Although this number varies each year, basically, if you reach the PGMOL, you can say you are in the top 1% of the country's officials. Something to be proud of.

"" You can say you were in the top 1%.

I only reached the National List. As detailed above, the SG2 was launched in 2016, and I was unsuccessful in my attempt to get accepted. Before SG2, all National List officials were able to officiate in Championship fixtures, which was always a personal highlight for me and, I'm sure, for other colleagues.

The PGMOL is not only concerned with appointments and personal rankings. There's a coaching element to membership as well. They want to help you improve, and during my time I had two coaches, Ralph Bone and Paul Canadine, both ex-Premier League assistant referees. Each had a number of officials to work with, so they would only see you in action occasionally, but whenever they did, their feedback was extremely helpful. My best season in terms of number of appointments was 2012/13, when Paul was my coach. We spoke weekly and he challenged me to seek constant improvement by demanding more of myself. It worked.

The PGMOL also employs a wide range of sports scientists, physiotherapists and sprint coaches. This set-up is designed to replicate the structure of a football club, which is all geared to improve performance. In addition to coaching, we had fitness advice and direction from sports scientist Simon Breivik, who is now Head of Fitness and Medicine. He gave us weekly fitness training plans to follow along with feedback on our training data. He was also responsible for the fitness tests every summer. As we have seen, this annual ordeal stretched you to the limit – and rightly so. The players were getting younger. You weren't, so you had to work harder to keep up with them. Harsh but fair.

For those who are seriously interested in our fitness test, there is a detailed section in the Appendix, but suffice it to say, you approached the test day with a feeling of dread and drove away with a sense of relief. Assuming you passed, that is. If you failed, you had two chances to retake, and if you failed both, you lost your place in the PGMOL. There were rumours that high-profile officials were allowed to take a retest in private. Failing in front of the rest of the group – as I found out myself – was a humiliating experience. But once passed, you were all set for the season ahead.

Appointments to fixtures were released to all officials on Monday afternoon at 4pm for games taking place the following weekend and midweek. The FA/PGMOL have a website called MOAS (Match Officials Administration System), and as soon as you got your email notification, you'd log in and confirm your availability. In addition, MOAS conveyed news bulletins and allowed you to manage your online diary, etc.

For a Saturday game, it was usual for the referee, as senior official, to ring on the Thursday to say hello and discuss anything relevant to that particular match. Whether I knew the referee well or not, these calls always helped with focus and team spirit.

Every game would typically mean some sort of involvement for an eight-day period. Sometimes, you'd have two appointments within the same time frame – Saturday and midweek. Match day was obviously pretty full on, and for those who'd like to see my typical weekly schedule in detail, it's laid out in the Appendix.

There was always the same shape to the match day, but each match was a unique event, which is what made it interesting of course. For it to be enjoyable and for you to play your part in it, you needed the consistent structure. The referee was always the team leader and gave match instructions before every game; their decisions were final (we'll get to VAR in the next chapter!), and predictably, every referee is an individual with their own personal style, their own quirks.

Some referees liked to talk a lot over the comms system, some weren't interested in pleasantries or attempts at humour: they just wanted information. Some delegated well and some liked to give every decision themselves. More than once, I saw an offence during a match and alerted the referee over the comms system, only to be told to keep my flag down as, quote: 'I don't want it.' Of course, I wasn't the only one to have seen the offence. The crowd behind me saw what I saw and couldn't understand why I wasn't signalling. Or forgive me for keeping my flag down. I never had the chance to explain...

Another integral member of the match day team is the assessor. An ex-official with plenty of experience, they are there to judge impartially the performance of each official. Some assessors had a reputation for harshness; others were felt to be a soft touch. Their assessments mattered, as their marks influenced your position in the Merit List, which in turn impacted your future games and your promotion and retention prospects.

> ❝ I vowed never to become an Assessor.

I vowed never to become an assessor. I saw it as a thankless task. If they received good marks, the officials would be happy, but only as confirmation that they had had a good game. Criticism and poor marks on the other hand could be devastating. What was worse was that the match day opinion was always subject to change after the assessor had viewed the DVD of the game when they got home. Smiling praise could turn overnight into a cold condemnation. Although I found many assessors a pleasure to work with, others were less supportive, and the day became more about them and how great they had been in their day than about the four people who had actually been out there officiating.

The PGMOL is a small world, and everyone knows everyone else. Sometimes colleagues moved on to become assessors, which could be slightly uncomfortable: suddenly, you're not quite on the same team anymore. I felt that the assessor is looking for the correct application of the Law, whereas the match officials are looking for the best application of the Law in the circumstance. An example of this is when a referee chooses to have a quiet word with a player who has just committed a foul instead of issuing a caution. The book might say that a yellow card was justified, but experience and player management might deem a talking-to sufficient.

Then there were reputations. There would be times when you were officiating with a colleague who was a 'name' – someone people had heard of, who was, in the largely anonymous world of match officials, famous. The assessor could find themselves in an awkward situation, and there were instances where I felt someone was judged on who they were, rather than on their performance on the day.

In my last season with the PGMOL, NL referees and assistant referees were organised into small groups for consistent appointments to games. These were known as Pentagons, as each referee would have five assistants working regularly with him. The idea was to create better teamwork and cooperation. This was great if you got on well with everyone in the group, but hard work if you didn't. A joke someone made at the last training day I attended was that there should be a 'Pentagon Transfer Window' for match officials...

CHAPTER CHALLENGES ANSWERS

1. *No – you can pass the ball and you can even backheel it. The ball must move forwards, however.*

2. *A penalty kick. Law says that if a player commits a physical offence inside the field of play against a match official, then play is restarted by the opponents with a direct free kick or a penalty kick if the offence took place inside the penalty area.*

CHAPTER 14

We Need to Talk about VAR

Cure-All or Confusion?

We really do need to talk about VAR. But before we do, we need to look at the Offside Law (Law 11). It's probably worth considering why the very idea of 'offside' came into existence in the first place. There was certainly no requirement for the concept when whole communities were rumbling from one end of town to the other in the traditional way. It was only when the concept of a defined playing area came in that the need for some regulation was recognised. Without some form of prohibition, the game would be spoiled by what was known as 'goal hanging': a player or players simply taking up a position in the goalmouth, crowding the goalkeeper and tapping the ball over the goal line. This was regarded as unsporting – 'sneaking' in Victorian slang. It was like hitting a man below the belt. But, as we have also seen, the draconian offside laws imposed by the early lawmakers had a detrimental effect on the development of the passing and dribbling skills that are now at the heart of the modern game.

Many of the English public schools had a reference to offside in their respective rules in the mid-1800s. Eton, for example, had in their 1847 Laws a provision that a player was not considered to be 'sneaking' if there were four or more opponents between him and the goal line.

CHAPTER CHALLENGES

1. *Can a player stand directly in front of an opponent who is taking a throw-in?*

2. *A substitute strikes another substitute from the other team off the field of play. The ball is in play when the incident happens. What is the correct restart after the offence has been punished?*

The 1863 Laws of the Game for the Football Association adopted a version of the Cambridge School Law that:

When a player has kicked the ball any one of the same side who is nearer to the

125

opponent's goal line is out of play and may not touch the ball himself nor in any way whatever prevent any other player from doing so until the ball has been played; but no player is out of play when the ball is kicked from behind the goal line.

The 'kick from behind the goal line' was the 1863 equivalent of a goal kick. This exception was necessary because every player on the attacking side would have otherwise been 'out of play' from such a kick.

At the first revision of the FA Laws, in February 1866, an important qualifier was added to soften the 'strict' offside law:

When a player has kicked the ball, any one of the same side who is nearer to the opponents' goal line is out of play, and may not touch the ball himself, nor in any way whatever prevent any other player from doing so, until the ball has been played, **unless there are at least three of his opponents between him and their own goal***; but no player is out of play when the ball is kicked from behind the goal line.*

The original Laws allowed players to be in an offside position even when in their own half. This happened rarely but it was possible to be offside in your own penalty area! In April 1906, a rule change was proposed that players in their own half couldn't be offside, and the proposal was passed by IFAB in June 1907.

At the IFAB meeting in 1894, a proposal to change the three-player offside rule to two players was rejected. It was rejected again in 1902, in 1913 and in 1914. After World War I, the proposal was rejected in 1922, 1923 and 1924. Finally, in 1925, IFAB approved the change, and the rule came into Law.

Goals were an immediate result, with the number rising from 4,700 in Football League games in 1924/25 to 6,373 in 1925/26 from the same number of games. A rise of 36%.

> Just being in an offside position is not an offence in itself.

The Offside Law remained unaltered for the next 65 years.

In 1990, IFAB decreed that an attacker level with the second-last defender is onside, whereas previously such a player had been considered offside.

In 2005, IFAB clarified that for offside purposes, the part of the player's head, body or feet closest to the defending team's goal line should be considered. The hands and arms were not considered, as they would not be used to play the ball.

In 2009, it was confirmed that a defender who leaves the field of play without the referee's permission would be ruled to be on the nearest boundary line for judging offside.

In 2016, it was clarified that a player on the halfway line itself is onside.

It's important to understand that just being in an offside position is not an offence in itself. A player commits an offside offence if they then become 'involved in active play', 'interfere with an opponent' or 'gain an advantage' by being in that position. That is when play is stopped and a free kick awarded.

An offside offence is not classed as a foul or misconduct and is only punishable by an indirect free kick. Judging offside is one of the assistant referees' primary duties. They raise their flags to signal the offside offence and then lower their flag to indicate the position of the restart. Ultimately the responsibility for the decision rests with the referee, who may overrule the offside signal if so minded. This can be felt as a put-down by the AR whose decision is dismissed and can leave him or her in a difficult position if the section of the crowd behind them saw the same thing.

ARs have many responsibilities, but the primary and most difficult one is judging offside, and it is the main thing they are judged on – not just how many decisions they get right, but more crucially, how many they get wrong. Of course, now there is VAR, which we will be looking at shortly. But prior to VAR, there was strong focus on helping ARs to get their decisions right.

The Flash Lag Effect

When judging offside, the AR must look at three things as a minimum: the player playing the ball, the player receiving the ball and the second rearmost defender (RMD). You only have two eyes, but you have three things to look at. Often, the AR will take a mental picture of the play at the moment the ball is played. Players are moving of course, often at high speed, and this makes the judgment of the offside decision even harder to get right. On our training days with the PGMOL, we practised offside decisions over and over again. We used video review to freeze the action so that our reviews were extremely accurate. The aim was perfection, but, hey, no one's perfect. We're human beings, equipped with one pair of eyes and a flag.

Hence the importance of the flash lag effect. This is the name given to the natural time delay covering the AR seeing all three elements – ball played, movement of the intended receiver and the second RMD. It's only a fraction of a second, but the time taken to process the picture in your mind creates a natural degree of error. Which needs to be compensated for.

Once the sports scientists started making us aware of FLE and helping us minimise its impact, the accuracy of our decision-making improved. The natural degree of error is dependent on the alertness of the AR and the speed that the attacker and defender cross over. Poor alertness and a high crossover speed increase the chance of an error.

A sprinter at the Olympics has a typical reaction time of 1/10 of a second. The same reaction time for an AR means that an attacking player can cover up to 1m. That is a long way when judging offside. Commentators looking at an action replay in slow motion claim that a player is 'clearly offside' if they are half a body ahead of the second RMD. A lot less than 1m.

> We had to train our brains to overrule our eyes.

So, the learning point for us as ARs was that, if an attacker looks 0.5m offside, then they were likely to have been level with the second RMD or better when the ball was played – i.e. they were onside.

We had to train our brains to overrule our eyes, which goes against a lifetime's experience.

The quicker the crossover of players, the greater the tolerance of distance could be applied, and the decision to keep the flag down would still be correct. A slow crossover speed would give a tolerance of approximately 30cm and a fast crossover speed would give a tolerance of potentially 2m.

Then there are special circumstances. The rule works in reverse when the attacking player is moving away from the goal line. Where players are in static positions, there is no crossover, so there is no degree of tolerance. The theory only applies when there is motion from the relevant players.

In training, we concentrated on three main areas: alertness – being on our toes, ready to move; focus – not being distracted and being in the right position to make the best judgment; and time – thinking for a split second to arrive at the correct decision. A delayed flag giving the right decision is always better than a quick but incorrect response. Fans and pundits want instant signals, but ARs have to resist the pressure for snap decisions. It's important to wait for the ball to reach its offside player destination, as it were, before the final judgment is made. Often, the best offside decisions are when the flag stays down. My best ones were…

But now of course we have VAR, so everything's straightforward and virtually perfect, isn't it? Well, that was certainly the intention, but as all football supporters can testify, it didn't work out quite that way.

In November 2020, the whole subject of offside and VAR came to a sharp focus when Patrick Bamford of Leeds had a goal against Crystal Palace ruled out for offside. As the ball was poked through, Bamford had his arm outstretched to signal where he wanted it to be played. Bamford duly received the ball and scored. VAR, however, showed Bamford's arm from the tricep down was in an offside position, and after a review the goal was disallowed.

This whole incident led to calls for the offside law to change to allow more advantage for attacking players. The change could be that if any part of your body is in an onside position, then you are judged to be onside. Currently, the opposite is true.

The whole idea behind VAR is to reduce the number of human errors that have in a big influence on match results. Sounds great in theory. Indeed, when VAR was first approved by IFAB and written into Law in 2018, the philosophy was 'minimal interference,

❝ Minimal interference, maximum benefit.

maximum benefit'. The main benefit gained by using VAR is that it would enable the correction of 'clear and obvious errors', and also the ability to correct 'serious missed incidents'.

The four categories of decisions that can be reviewed by VAR currently are:

· Goal/no goal – attacking team commits an offence, ball out of play, ball entering goal, offside, handball, offences and encroachment during penalty kicks.

· Penalty/no penalty – attacking team commits an offence, ball out of play, location of offence, incorrect awarding, offence not penalised.

· Direct red card – denial of obvious goal-scoring opportunity, serious foul play, violent conduct/biting/spitting, using offensive/insulting/abusive language or gestures. All straight red cards are subject to review.

· Mistaken identity in awarding a red or yellow card.

The VAR team will check every on-field referee decision that comes under any of the four categories. A 'silent check' is where no error is detected and the referee is given the all-clear. At other times, VAR checks a possible error and the game is delayed while the check takes place. If an error is found by VAR, then the referee has three options:

· Decision overturned on advice of VAR

· On-field review (OFR) recommended

· Referee chooses to ignore VAR advice

In matters of fact, a decision can be changed without an OFR. When there is a subjective decision to make, then an OFR is recommended. The referee ultimately is the referee and if they wish, they can ignore VAR advice altogether.

The referee signals an OFR by indicating a video screen. The review takes place in a designated referee review area (RRA) next to the field of play. It is also in public view to ensure transparency. The referee is able to view several video replays from different camera angles to help them arrive at their decision.

If a player or team official excessively makes the TV signal, they may be cautioned; and also if they enter the RRA, they will be cautioned.

The assistant video assistant referee (AVAR) is appointed to assist the VAR in the video operation room. They are there to watch the live action on the field while the VAR is undertaking a 'check' or a 'review', to keep a record of reviewable incidents, and to communicate the outcome of a review to broadcasters.

The idea of VAR is believed to have come from Holland in the early 2010s. The system was tested from 2012 onwards. In the early days, the then-FIFA president, Sepp Blatter, was against introducing new technology to the game. However, when Gianni Infantino became president, the proposal was warmly received. The first live trial of the VAR system was in July 2016 in a friendly match between PSV and FC Eindhoven.

During the testing period, it became clear that VAR decisions needed to be clearly communicated to the players, the watching public inside the stadium, and on TV.

In January 2018, VAR was trialled for the first time in England in the FA Cup game between Brighton and Hove Albion and Crystal Palace. The Premier League introduced VAR from the 2019/20 season onwards.

In the build-up to VAR becoming commonplace, there were many commentators who were insistent that it would only be a benefit and any delay to the game would be a matter of seconds. There has been, however, plenty of criticism of VAR since its introduction, e.g.:

2017 FIFA Confederations Cup – VAR accused of 'creating as much confusion as clarity'.

2018 A-League grand final – VAR suffered a technical malfunction which prevented the assistant referee from viewing the replay.

VAR accused in *The Guardian* of lacking clarity and consistency. Effective for factual decisions but less good for subjective decisions.

VAR accused of a lack of transparency and still requiring a human judgment to be made.

VAR accused in the Premier League of being confusing for team officials and supporters due to inconsistent decision-making.

Handball, offside or penalty decision... Over three years after the VAR system was introduced into the Premier League, every club, every manager, players and fans have all raged at the system. You cannot put the toothpaste back into the tube, however, so we have to accept that VAR is a fact of football life.

But what can be done to make it better? Some suggestions to consider:

Greater training for VAR officials to obtain greater consistency regarding interventions over 'clear and obvious errors'.

Recruit dedicated VAR officials – use former League officials – rather than using current match officials.

Annual assessment for VAR officials.

Referee and VAR teams to be developed and appointed to fixtures together regularly.

AR to be instructed to flag for offside incidents when clear to see rather than waiting for VAR.

Referee and VAR dialogue open to the stadium/TV audiences.

Each VAR intervention to require pitch-side review from the match referee.

VAR has been in use in the Premier League for four years now and the disputes about its use still rage. The explosions of anger about VAR over the first weekend in September this season brought matters to a head. West Ham were outraged over a disallowed goal against Chelsea, Newcastle United were furious about a disallowed goal against Crystal Palace and Leeds United were angry because they were not awarded a penalty against Brentford. On the same day Michael Oliver stuck to his original decision to award Nottingham Forest a penalty against Bournemouth and was widely praised for not being swayed by VAR.

That evening on Match of the Day Alan Shearer called the decisions 'beyond terrible' and 'shocking'. Alan went on to say, 'far too many errors, VAR is not the problem, it is the people who are running it.'

Monday morning brought further comment with former PGMOL boss Keith Hackett claiming that referees would be feeling 'let down' by VAR and that they are being 'hung out to dry' by the mistakes.

The PGMOL later conceded that the decisions in the matches at Newcastle and Chelsea were errors.

The new Chief Refereeing Officer at the PGMOL is Howard Webb and one of the tasks he faces is to improve VAR and restore confidence in the system.

As everyone now concedes, VAR is a work-in-progress. It seems there are no easy fixes, however smart the technology gets.

CHAPTER CHALLENGES ANSWERS

1. *No – they must be 2m away from the part of the touchline where the throw will be taken from.*

2. *A direct free kick taken from the boundary line nearest to where the offence occurred – a penalty kick if the penalty area is the nearest boundary line.*

PART 5

THE WIDER VIEW

CHAPTER 15

Match Officials in World Cup History

The Hand of God, etc.

But let's go back to the pre-technology era and remind ourselves why VAR became inevitable. As we head towards the greatest sporting show on earth, here are some characters and episodes from the World Cup archive.

Players and fans all over the world love the tournament and the thrills it brings. It's also a bonus that the inevitable controversies remain talking points for many years to come. The teams spend the best part of a year qualifying and get there on merit. The other on-field participants – the referees and assistant referees – are carefully selected by committee, are supposed to be at the top of their game, are desperate to perform well, and are keen not to be the centre of attention. Sometimes, however, the story does involve the assistant referee caught in the harsh glare of the spotlight.

Before we reflect on some unfortunate moments in the limelight, it's worth noting just how successful England is regarding the appointments of assistant referees to the World Cup final itself. The score line here is in fact:

Argentina 5 England 4

Only Argentina has supplied more assistants to the final than England, up to and including the final in 2018. So, who are our Fab Four?

CHAPTER CHALLENGES

1. *At a corner kick, a player from the defending team stands 10 yards/9.15m away from the corner flag to try to block the ball when the kick is taken. Is this allowed?*

2. *A player scores a goal and the referee blows for half time instead of a kick-off. The players are still on the field of play when the AR tells the referee that the goal was scored with a deliberate handball. What should the referee do?*

Mark Warren

Mark worked as a police officer and began refereeing in 1978. He became an international AR in 1994 and ran the line at the 1998 World Cup final in France, where the host country beat Brazil 3-0.

Phil Sharp

Phil began refereeing as part of the DoE Award Scheme and reached the FIFA list in 1997. He ran the line at the 2002 World Cup final in Japan, where Brazil beat Germany 2-0. I have had the pleasure of officiating with Phil on many occasions.

Mike Mullarkey

Mike started refereeing aged 17 and formed a team unit with Howard Webb and Darren Cann. He ran the line at the 2010 World Cup final in South Africa, where Spain beat Holland 1-0.

Darren Cann

Darren began refereeing in 1991 and quickly rose through the ranks. I had the pleasure of officiating with Darren but couldn't keep up with him as he soared to the pinnacle of officiating in the 2010 World Cup final in South Africa, where Spain beat Holland 1-0.

In 2011, the work of Mike and Darren, along with Howard Webb, was recognised when they were all awarded the PFA Special Merit Award. This is the only time to date a refereeing team have received such an honour.

But on the downside...

Notable incidents in and around the World Cup where the assistant referee has had some involvement include the following:

England 1966 – England 4 West Germany 2

England's third goal. Did the shot from Geoff Hurst go over the line? Yes? No? Will we ever know for sure? Well, in 2016, Sky Sports used modern technology to analyse the incident and concluded that the ball did cross the line.

The linesman who gave the goal was not Russian, as many people believe. He was actually from Azerbaijan and his name was Tofiq Bahramov.

After his death in 1993, Azerbaijan's then national stadium was renamed the Tofiq Bahramov Republican Stadium in his honour.

Spain 1982 – France 4 Kuwait 1

In England's group, the game between Kuwait and France descended into farce in the second half.

Alain Giresse scored a fourth goal for France, but the goal was met with protests from the Kuwait players. They claimed they had heard a whistle, which they thought was from the referee, so they stopped playing.

Sheikh Fahad Al-Ahmed Al-Jaber Al-Sabah, prince of Kuwait and also president of the nation's football association, rushed onto the pitch to remonstrate with the referee.

Soviet referee Miroslav Stupar consulted with his two linesmen and then decided to rule out the goal – this of course made the French players furious. After a while, order was restored, the game continued, and France won 4-1 in the end.

Referee Stupar was banned from officiating thereafter.

South Africa 2010 – Germany 4 England 1

This was the game where the 'ghost' goal by Frank Lampard led to the initiative for goal line technology. England were 2-1 down when the shot from Frank hit the bar and bounced over the line. TV replays were instant and conclusive.

The assistant referee at that end of the field was Mauricio Espinosa, and he later admitted that he was caught out by the speed of the shot. He was unable to see that the ball had crossed the line from his position, and he gave no signal. There was no whistle, so the play continued, and referee Jorge Larrionda didn't award a goal. England went on to lose 4-1.

" Sepp Blatter offered a fulsome apology.

As a result of this glaring failure, for which Sepp Blatter offered a fulsome apology, the pursuit of goal line technology began in earnest, and in July 2012 the International Football Association (IFAB) officially approved its use.

Mexico 1986 – Argentina 2 England 1 'The Hand of God'

Diego Maradona handled the ball to score for Argentina, and as he celebrated, the England players surrounded the referee, Ali Bin Nasser of Tunisia, protesting against the goal being given. However, neither he nor his linesman, Bogdan Dochev, had spotted the offence, and the controversial goal stood.

TV replays and photographs clearly showed that Maradona had handled the ball. Maradona said after the game, 'I was waiting for my teammates to embrace me, and no one came... I told them, "Come hug me, or the referee isn't going to allow it."'

The photographs were so clear that there was no hiding place for the officials. Bin Nasser and Dochev blamed each other for the error. 'I was waiting for Dochev to give me a hint of what exactly happened, but he didn't signal for a handball,' Bin Nasser said years later.

In 2007, in an interview, Dochev allegedly admitted that he had seen what Maradona had done, but it happened too fast for him to give any indication. Ultimately though, he also claimed that the final decision rests with the referee.

How long will it be until we have another really controversial issue to get worked up about? Probably not too long...

The next World Cup is in Qatar in November/December 2022. Even in the qualifying matches, the unusual stories regarding some of the assistant referees continue... In January 2022, the qualifying game between Chile and Argentina contained a very surreal circumstance.

The assistant referees, Fabricio Vilarinho and Rodrigo Figueiredo, realised on arrival at the stadium that they had forgotten to bring their flags and had to find an alternative as a matter of urgency. Images showed the pair using hi-vis jackets attached to broom handles! As the saying has it, necessity is the mother of invention...

FIFA is keen to introduce 'semi-automated offside' calls at the tournament in Qatar. IFAB propose to approve the use of skeletal modelling by Hawk-Eye to determine the exact positions of players when the ball is played. A total of 29 points of the body of each player are tracked by the algorithm to provide the feedback on positions. It is accurate to within 4cm, and if a player is deemed offside, a signal will be sent electronically to officials, enabling calls within seconds.

> **FIFA is keen to introduce "semi-automated offside".**

But it also gives time for the VAR to quickly assess if an 'offside' player is not interfering with play, preventing the whistle being blown incorrectly to stop a legitimate goal from being scored.

The plan is to roll this out in the Premier League from the start of season 2023/24.

CHAPTER CHALLENGES ANSWERS

1. *No – the defending players need to be 10 yards/9.15m away from the corner arc and not the flag.*

2. *Disallow the goal, show the offender a yellow card and go to the dressing room for half time.*

CHAPTER 16

Where Are We Now and Where Are We Going?

A Brighter Future with Some Changes to the Game

We're all fans of the beautiful game. Most of us have life-long commitments to one – or possibly two – teams. We all watch them avidly, whether in person or on the screen. We all have moments of triumph and taste the depths of despair. No one likes watching their team lose, but what people hate most is their team losing because of an error by the officials, including VAR. Managers on the touchline swing aggressively to confront the fourth official for explanations of the inexplicable; players roll their eyes, laugh sarcastically; and the fans in the ground go mad. The good news is that officials really hate getting decisions wrong and spend a lot of time training to get them right. The same goes for VAR. The rules are not set in stone. There is an inevitable tendency to review and improve any innovation, especially one so massively significant.

But what of the game as a whole? Talk to any football fan and he or she will have something they'd like to change. And I'm no different. So, as we near the end of this personal saga, I'm going to offer a few suggestions based on my experience, both as an official and as supporter. It'll be pretty obvious what the motivation is behind each one

CHAPTER CHALLENGES

1. *Can an injured player who is off the field of play being treated at the final whistle take part in a penalty shoot-out?*

2. *An attacker has created a promising attack but is recklessly fouled. The referee plays advantage and the attacking team scores a goal. What is the correct sanction to the offending player?*

of them: to remove an irritating feature of the current game – things that slow the game down or are clearly against the spirit of football. We'll start, perhaps predictably, with a few Law changes:

Offside offence only possible in opponents' penalty area.

All free kicks to be direct.

Goalkeepers not permitted to leave their own penalty area.

No passes allowed to the goalkeeper from outside the penalty area.

> ❝ No one likes watching their team lose.

Simulation should be upgraded to serious foul play. Sanction to be raised to red card.

Sin bins to replace all non-contact caution offences.

Throw-in in own half may only be thrown forwards.

Free kicks may be taken to self (as in rugby union).

No substitutes allowed in the last ten minutes of the game.

And here are some other suggestions:

Two referees per game – one in each half of the pitch.

External timekeeper – each game to be 60 minutes of ball-in-play time.

Football season to run from February to November below National League level.

World Cup to be held in July rather than June, becoming a pre-season tournament rather than an end of season tournament.

> ❝ Officials really hate getting the decisions wrong.

Captains to have one appeal to the referee each half.

Technical area protocols – all occupants allowed to stand. However, leaving the area results in immediate sending off.

Bonus points for winning margins, e.g. a three-goal margin gains four points.

Four points for an away win.

Injured players to leave the field of play for minimum of five minutes.

Replace League Cup with Divisional Cups for Premier League down to League 2.

FA Cup winners guaranteed place in Champions League the following season.

FA Cup ties – the higher ranked team at time of the draw plays away from home.

Relegation play-offs in each League. Bottom two clubs relegated automatically, but third and fourth from bottom play each other for survival.

Caution for foul play to the team not the individual player. Three cautions in a game = one player dismissed. Captain decides which player is sanctioned.

Players only eligible for country of birth in international competitions.

Salary maximum budget per club per season.

Ticket prices capped for spectators:
Premier League – £20
Championship – £16
League 1 – £12
League 2 – £10
Non-League – £5

Thankfully, in the 21st century, it is perfectly normal for anyone and everyone to take part in football. The game is for everyone. This was not always the case however, and in December 1921 the FA actually banned females from playing football. The ban meant that clubs belonging to the associations were 'to refuse the use of their grounds for such matches'.

It took 50 years for the ban to be lifted, and in 1971 women's football was back. The revival took place all around the world, and in 1984 the first European Championship was held, and the winners were Sweden, who beat England in a two-legged final. The second leg was played at Kenilworth Road and England were beaten on 4-3 on penalties. The first World Cup was held in China 1991 with the USA beating Norway 2-1 in the final. With the

WSL in place in England since 2011, women's football continues to grow in popularity, gain more media coverage and attract more sponsors.

Barcelona women's team have enjoyed crowds of over 90,000, and in England this summer, as we all know, the Lionesses won the European Championships on home soil. England's first trophy since 1966 meant that, after 56 years, it felt like football finally had come home again. On that lovely Sunday evening in July, I was one of the lucky 87,192 supporters inside Wembley who witnessed England win the trophy, and when Chloe Kelly scored the winning goal, the stadium erupted. After this record-breaking tournament, women's football is surely destined to go to a whole new level, which would be a fitting legacy for the amazing English squad.

Bobby Moore did it in 1966, and now in 2022 Leah Williamson has done it too. England – European Champions... Sounds good, doesn't it!

And it isn't just the players on the field that have been breaking down barriers. Remember Wendy Toms? She was the first female assistant referee in the Football League in 1994 and also the first female assistant referee in the Premier League in 1997. Wendy also made the FIFA List in 2000.

During my time in the PGMOL, I had the chance to officiate in matches with Sian Massey-Ellis and Amy Fearn. I found them both to be extremely talented, completely dedicated, and full of warm enthusiasm for the game. Sian and Amy proved themselves to be excellent officials who were setting a great example for others to follow.

Football really is for everyone. In my opinion, that is why it is the greatest game on earth.

CHAPTER CHALLENGES ANSWERS

1. *Yes – any player who is temporarily off the field for a valid reason (injury, changing equipment, etc....) is allowed to take part. However, a substitution cannot be made after the final whistle.*

2. *Yellow card – the team were not denied an obvious goal-scoring opportunity.*

CHAPTER 17

Match-Fixing and the Power of Money

Stuff Happens

I am sometimes asked about match-fixing. A quick Q&A:

Do I have any evidence of match-fixing in football? No.

Am I aware of any matches being fixed? No.

Was I ever asked to fix a match while on the National List? No.

Do I think it is possible to fix a football match? No.

When it was alleged that Bruce Grobbelaar fixed a match in 1994, my reaction was: 'Okay, he might be able to let a goal in, but how would he stop Ian Rush scoring at the other end?' In other words, it is virtually impossible for an individual player to fix a match. And of course, the more team members are involved, the greater the likelihood that the plot would be discovered.

What is possible, however, is 'spot fixing', where an individual can engineer a specific incident in a game on which money can be wagered and for which they can be paid. And that would apply in the case of match officials too, and even those not personally involved in the match at all.

There is no proof regarding any of the following theories, but there are certainly conspiracy theorists out there who would believe any or all have occurred.

Bets placed on the time of the first throw-in. If it's within the first 30 seconds, all the culprit has to do is kick the ball out of play from the kick-off.

CHAPTER CHALLENGES

1. *An attacking player is standing in the opponent's half of the field of play and closer to the halfway line than the defender marking them. The ball is passed to the attacking player by a teammate and the assistant referee immediately raises their flag to signal an offside offence. How is this the correct decision?*

2. *Can a player take a free kick with two feet?*

Floodlights 'failing' and the match being abandoned. What odds would you get on that? In November 1997, the floodlights failed when West Ham were playing Crystal Palace in the Premier League. A large pay-out was made to an Asian betting syndicate which had bet on exactly that eventuality. The same thing happened a month later in a match between Wimbledon and Arsenal, but suspicions were raised by this, and when the third attempt was made, at a Charlton v Liverpool game, the perpetrators were caught, tried and sent to prison.

> " How would he stop Ian Rush scoring at the other end?

There are also opportunities for less complicated incidents, like a player celebrating a goal in front of a specified advertising board, or injured players parking themselves near a particular advert to receive their medical attention. (Though, with the rolling electronic advertising boards used at the upper-tier stadiums, that ploy has ceased to be an option.)

Then there are the occasions when a player might do something deliberately, not for a back-hander, but to effect a preferred personal outcome. Players might be interested in getting a yellow card just before Christmas if it meant suspension for the Boxing Day match and thus extending Christmas with the family.

No one's going to admit to that sort of thing. Except that the England captain, David Beckham, did in October 2004. Obviously, this had nothing to do with Christmas, but he confirmed that he had intentionally got himself booked in a game against Wales knowing that he would miss the next match away to Azerbaijan due to an injury. The yellow card in the Wales game meant he was suspended for the next England game. In his own words, and quoted in *The Guardian* newspaper, he 'got the yellow card out of the way'. That might have been an unwise confession, but it was a million miles away from match-fixing.

> " Obviously this had nothing to do with Christmas.

But the possibility of corruption in the game was taken very seriously by the PGMOL. Those of us on the National List were subject to several interdictions. For a start, there was a blanket ban on officials betting on football. We were actively discouraged from using social media – Facebook, Twitter, etc. – to discuss games, make predictions, or in any way be seen to be involved in the games in which we officiated. Mobile phones were not to be used after a certain time on match days.

Along with repeated warnings regarding personal betting, we were required to report any inappropriate contacts that people attempted to make. Appointments to matches were only released on Monday for the following weekend, but if any irregular betting patterns should show up, there could be a last-minute reallocation of officials as deemed appropriate.

Football, as we know, is a multi-billion global sport. And where there's vast amounts of money, there is always likely to be corruption. Take, as one example, the final Championship play-off to decide which of two teams should go up to the Premier League. This is now recognised as the single most 'valuable' football match in the world. Promotion to the Premier League is reckoned currently to be worth around £170 million. I should say immediately that there has never been any suggestion that anyone involved in this key match over the years has been suborned or bribed to affect the result.

But there have undoubtedly been examples of match-fixing over the years, and inevitably, whenever it happens, it is a huge news story. In 2013, *The Sun on Sunday* secretly filmed a conversation with an ex-Portsmouth player, Sam Sodje, who told an undercover reporter that he could arrange red or yellow cards for cash. He cited one incident in a League 1 game against Oldham Athletic where he punched an opponent so as to get a red card. He charged £70,000 for that.

Unsavoury and clearly criminal, that incident and others like it would not have had much impact on results. Over years, there have been cases of much more serious corruption in football.

In 1964, a betting ring involving several Football League players was uncovered. Players from Sheffield Wednesday were found to have been deliberately losing matches. What they hadn't betted on was being caught and banned from the game for the rest of their lives.

> " Milan had licence to kick Leeds players.

Ten years on, in May 1973, Leeds United met AC Milan in the European Cup Winners final hosted by Greece. The Greek referee, Christos Michas, was the centre of attention here, as questionable decisions became the running story of the match. BBC commentator Barry Davies shared his doubts about some of the decisions with his audience. One of these resulted in Milan scoring from a free kick. For most of the match, it looked very much as though Milan had licence to kick Leeds players without sanction, and two obvious fouls in the penalty area against Trevor Cherry and Mick Jones were waved away by the referee. The game ended 1-0 to AC Milan, but the final whistle brought a chorus of boos and catcalls from the Greek crowd.

There were claims that Michas was bribed by Milan, and it was later revealed that he had flown in on the same flight as the Milan team. The Greek FA investigated and he was subsequently banned for life by UEFA.

A similar scandal occurred when Anderlecht played Nottingham Forest in a UEFA Cup semi-final in April 1984. Referee Emilio Guruceta Muro was revealed to have accepted a bribe of £18,000 from the former Anderlecht president, Constant Vanden Stock. The disgraceful truth was exposed after two people were arrested for apparently blackmailing Anderlecht, claiming to have secretly taped conversations with Muro and demanding hundreds of thousands of pounds for their silence. Anderlecht won the game 3-0 and the tie 3-2 on aggregate.

A German referee, Robert Hoyzer, was found guilty in 2005 of fixing and betting on matches in which he officiated. He was banned for life and sentenced to a spell in prison.

My own experience of possible skulduggery was, happily, limited. I once gave a yellow card in response to an offence which seemed somehow 'staged', and when I discussed it with colleagues, there was a suggestion that the offender might have had an ulterior motive in behaving as he had. Was there any proof? Absolutely none. But it did make me think.

As did being asked to give evidence as a witness to an investigation into a game between Colchester United and Preston North End in 2013. For two hours one evening that summer, an officer from the CPS took a statement from me to help building up 'the case'. My confidence in the process took a bit of a blow when, at the end of the interview, the officer handed me some notes taken from a previous conversation with a colleague. These were supposed to be evidence and therefore confidential. I pointed this out and he apologised and gave me the correct notes to read.

Was this a deliberate mistake to test me? I have no idea, but I am glad I didn't read anything I shouldn't have seen. Several months later, I heard that charges against the suspects were being dropped due to lack of evidence.

So, stuff happens. There are proven instances of match officials succumbing to temptation and risking the loss of their reputation, profession and even liberty. But is it widespread? I don't believe so.

Rigging a game or any part of it would be risky, and the bigger the interference in the game, the greater the risk of exposure. As with any criminal activity, the more people there are in the know, the greater chance of exposure. It just needs one person going a bit large down the pub for the story to leak out.

As far as the match officials are concerned, their behaviour is highly regulated and monitored. You're hauled over the coals for getting the closest of calls wrong, so obvious errors would come under the most severe scrutiny.

The security operation conducted by the FA, the Premier League, the EFL and the PGMOL make it almost impossible for match-fixing to take place – certainly not on a regular basis. The absence of a scandal in England is proof of that.

One final thought: the amount of money a match official would have to ask for to make the risk worthwhile would probably price them out of the market. As we've seen, getting caught would involve a lifetime ban, irreversible reputational damage, possibly prison. How much would it take to compensate you for all of that?

Of course, I have been discussing low-entry corruption. Higher up the game's pyramid where the money gets ridiculous, there are persistent rumours of corruption on an epic scale. But that is very much above my pay grade.

CHAPTER CHALLENGES ANSWERS

1. *Law 11 states that a player is in an offside position if they are nearer the goal line than the second last opponent. For this particular decision to be correct, the goalkeeper has to have taken up a position in the opponent's half to join in an attack. This would leave only one opponent between the attacking player and the goal line.*

2. *Yes – but only if both feet are used simultaneously.*

PART 6

EXTRA TIME

CHAPTER 18

So you think you know about football?
– have a go at Gavin's Football Quiz

Answers on page 160

The Questions

1. What is taken to the FA Cup final every year but never used?

2. Which team held the FA Cup for the longest time?

3. Sunderland did it in 1979, Villa did it in 1981... Who did it in 1980?

4. In the 1947 FA Cup final, what happened during the match for the second consecutive year that has never happened since?

5. Name the two British players who have won four or more European Cups/Champions Leagues?

6. When was the first game played in which the players had numbers on their shirts?

7. Which Premier League winning player has a surname made entirely of Roman numerals?

8. Which player has played a first team game for Manchester United, Manchester City, Everton and Liverpool?

9. Who are the only non-League team to play against England?

10. Who is the odd one out – Alan Brazil, Stephen Ireland, Joe Jordan, Jason Scotland or Mike England?

11. Which footballer appeared on the same episode of *Top of the Pops* twice with two different groups?

12. Which English professional club has a name where the first five letters are consonants?

13. Which English professional club is not named after a place on the map?

14. Who were the last team elected to the Football League?

15. Who was the first player to win both the FA Trophy and the FA Cup?

16. Who are the first ex-Premier League team to be relegated to the non-League?

17. Which team were holders of the Europa League and Champions League at the same time?

18. Who was the first Englishman to manage at a World Cup final?

19. How was the 1968 European Championship semi-final between Italy and the Soviet Union decided?

20. Which team in the EFL have a name where you can't colour in any of the letters?

21. Who are the only team in the UK with the letters A, B, C, D and E in their name?

22. Who once played for both Wales and Bayern Munich on the same day?

23. Which three England captains have played for Scunthorpe United?

24. Which two national teams have an elephant on their badges?

25. Which were the first five national leagues to adopt three points for a win?

CHAPTER 19

Fun Stuff

Jokes, Quotes and Anecdotes

Q - Who would make the perfect referee?
A - Snow White – she is the fairest of them all.

Q - Why did the referee get sacked from his job at the Home Office?
A - Supposedly, he was a whistle-blower.

In the middle of the game, the referee suddenly blows his whistle to stop play when he sees a long funeral procession on the road that runs alongside the field. He closes his eyes and bows his head in prayer.

'Wow,' said the yellow-carded striker. 'That is the most thoughtful and touching thing I've ever seen. You truly are a kind man. I'll never think badly of a referee again.'

The referee replies, 'Thanks, lad, we were married nearly 30 years.'

In the first half of a big game, a tricky young winger dribbles the ball past a big, burly and experienced defender.

The winger is jogging past the defender a moment later when the defender growls at him, 'If you come near me again, I'll break your legs!'

In a state of shock, the winger looks around and sees the referee close by... He immediately complains to the referee – 'Did you hear that!?'

'Yes, I did,' replied the referee. 'But I think he was talking to you...!'

'Having one child makes you a parent... Having two makes you a referee.'
David Frost

'The trouble with referees is that they know the rules, but they do not know the game.' **Bill Shankly**

'I was waiting for my teammates to embrace me, and no one came... I told them, "Come hug me or the referee isn't going to allow it."' **Diego Maradona**

'If you're good enough, the referee doesn't matter.' **Jock Stein**

'I think you and the referee were in a minority of one, Billy.' **Jimmy Armfield**

'I do swear a lot, but the advantage of having played abroad is that I can choose a different language from the referees.' **Jürgen Klinsmann**

'McCarthy shakes his head in agreement with the referee.' **Martin Tyler**

'When I saw Rijkaard entering the referee's dressing room, I couldn't believe it. When Didier Drogba was sent off, I wasn't surprised.' **José Mourinho**

'I never comment on referees and I'm not going to break the habit of a lifetime for that prat.' **Ron Atkinson**

'Referees don't come down here with a particular flavoured shirt on.' **Steve Coppell**

'On the field during a match are 22 cheats and a conman.' **Anon.**

CHAPTER 20

Poetry in Motion
That Goal

However exasperating Paul Gascoigne could be, there was no denying his fabulous footballing talent. He had a great Euro 1996, and his goal against Scotland was an example of that rare phenomenon, 'poetry in motion'.

That Goal

For Andrew Bolton, who has carried around a copy of it for more than 25 years.

How good was Gascoigne's goal?
As good as the tarts the knave stole,
As good as a cream-stuffed profiterole
Wolfed whole.

And how good was his left foot?
Better than the one in his right boot
With which he elected to shoot?
That's moot.

Suffice it to say his first touch
Left little but straws at which to clutch.
Too good for the Scots? – Or the Dutch?
Oh, much.

So talk not of the haircut,
The incipient beer-gut
Or of the man's being a fruit-and-nut
Case, but

Savour simply the sublime control,
Like angels performing rock'n'roll
On the dance floor of a pinhead. Extol
That goal!

The Guardian, June 1996

Gavin's Football Quiz – Answers

1. The losers' ribbons.

2. Portsmouth – 1939-1946 due to World War II.

3. Trevor Brooking – scored the winner in the FA Cup final.

4. The ball burst – poor leather quality after World War II.

5. Phil Neal – 1977, 1978, 1981, 1984; and Gareth Bale – 2014, 2016, 2017, 2018, 2022.

6. 25th August 1928 – Sheffield Wednesday v Arsenal. Wednesday wore 1-11 and Arsenal 12-22.

7. Nemanja Vidić – V=5, I=1, D=500, C=100.

8. Peter Beardsley.

9. Aylesbury United – on 4th June 1988 in a friendly prior to Euro '88.

10. Stephen Ireland is the only one to play for the country of his name – Brazil and Jordan played for Scotland, England played for Wales, and Scotland played for Trinidad and Tobago.

11. Steve Archibald – in 1982 with the Scotland World Cup Squad/B. A. Robertson – 'We have a Dream'; and then with Tottenham Hotspur/Chas & Dave – 'Tottenham, Tottenham'.

12. Crystal Palace.

13. Port Vale – the name is a reference to a valley of ports on the Trent and Mersey Canal.

14. Wigan Athletic – in 1978, replacing Southport.

15. Milija Aleksic – with Stafford Rangers in 1972 and Tottenham Hotspur in 1981.

16. Oldham Athletic – relegated from the EFL in 2022.

17. Chelsea – 2012 Champions League winners and 2013 Europa League winners ten days before the 2013 Champions League final.

18. George Raynor – Sweden in 1958.

19. A coin toss.

20. Hull City – no closed letters.

21. Cowdenbeath FC.

22. Mark Hughes – in 1987.

23. Kevin Keegan, Ray Clemence, Sir Ian Botham.

24. Ivory Coast and Thailand.

25. England in 1981, Israel in 1982, New Zealand in 1983, Iceland in 1984 and Northern Ireland in 1986.

APPENDIX

Being a Match Official – the Detail

PGMOL summer fitness test
The annual fitness test has now altered, but in my time, it involved four elements:

- Blood pressure reading taken by a doctor or medical professional
- Body fat analysis
- Sprints:
    6x40m in 6.0 seconds or less
    1.5m dynamic start
    Trip gate timing
- Repeated HI running:
    150m in 30 seconds
    40 seconds recovery to walk 50m
    Repeat for a total of 20 runs – 10 laps of a track
    The HI running element has now been adjusted to 75m runs x40 with 25m recovery walk.

My typical weekly PGMOL schedule during the season
My typical training week/match day schedule was as follows...
In addition I also went to work!

- **Monday** – appointment notification
- Gym session – 60 mins

- **Tuesday** – confirm appointment with home club
- High Intensity running at 85+% HR for 20 minutes
- Recovery session

- **Wednesday** – Running at 65% HR for 20 minutes

- **Thursday** – speak to referee
- Sprinting and agility session – 30 minutes

- **Friday** – Rest day
- Pack kit bag
- Plan journey to ground
- Study previous assessments from assessor
- Look at past game videos for both clubs
- Visit club websites for latest news – injuries, suspensions, etc.

Saturday – match day

Big breakfast, dress in PGMOL suit and tie

Leave home between 9-10am depending on journey ahead

12 noon – arrive at ground, meet colleagues and assessor, bags to dressing rooms, look at pitch, head to lounge area

1.30pm – briefing in dressing room from club safety supervisor and/or police

1.45pm – team sheets arrive from club officials and captains

1.50pm – match instructions from referee

2.00pm – get changed

2.30pm – warm up on pitch

2.53pm – ring bell to alert teams

2.55pm – lead out teams

3.00pm – kick-off

4.50pm – match ends

5.00pm – shower and change

5.10pm – debrief with assessor

5.45pm – back to car for journey home

7.30pm – arrive home, unpack kit bag

My typical distance that I covered was approx. 5km per game as AR = 1,200-1,500 calories burned.

Referees can often cover 10km per game and burn 2,000+ calories.

Sunday

8.00am – active recovery session in gym

Telephone call from assessor to discuss KMDs (Key Match Decisions)

Repeat day plans as previous week

Tuesday – receive assessment from assessor

Contents of a kit bag

Match official kit bag contents – professional game level:

Shirts x8 – 4 colours, long and short sleeve for each

Shorts x2

Socks x2

Undershirt x2

Undershorts x2

Warm-up top – dry weather

Warm-up top – wet weather

Tracksuit trousers

Rain jacket

3 pairs of boots – pimples, short stud, long stud
Communication system
AR flags and fourth official stick
LOAF book
Accessories bag:
Whistles x3
Notebook
Match record cards
Red/yellow cards
HR monitor
Stopwatch
Pencils
Coins

Costs of an assistant referee flag

Full set of buzzer flags and fourth official stick. RRP approx. £585.00.
Mid-range flag set. RRP £30.00.

Match official earnings

The fees paid to match officials don't compare in any way to the amount paid to the players. The crowd are there to watch the players and not the match officials; however, the game won't take place without the match officials' team.

In my time on the National List, I earned typically £8,000 a year, and as time passes the match officials fees rise year on year.

Select Group referees are now full time for the PGMOL, so it is only fair that they are compensated on a full-time basis. Typically, a Premier League referee can now earn anything from £38,000 to £70,000 per year. This is due to the scale of match fees where a referee is paid £1,500 per game and an assistant referee is paid £850 per game.

The officials who are also on the UEFA List and cover games in the Champions League, Europa League and Conference League will boost their earnings substantially.

Should the match officials be paid more? I believe so. The dedication to reach that professional level and the expectations on performance are more than enough reasons to justify a pay scale that reflect the role. And its importance.

Would more money improve performance? Maybe. It would certainly pay for thorough preparation for each game. I must say though, that when I was sprinting as fast as possible along the line chasing the players, I certainly wasn't thinking about money! And no amount of money could have made me run faster... I was already going as fast as I could!

The PGMOL is funded by the FA, the Premier League and the EFL. These three organisations generate plenty of revenue from commercial contracts, so going forward, finance really shouldn't be too much of an issue.

Life on the line as a career option? Definitely.

Links to YouTube clips

The Barron Knights – 'Hatters, Hatters'
https://www.youtube.com/watch?v=LDlj2T-cyIY

1966 World Cup Final – England v West Germany
https://www.youtube.com/watch?v=C0aK2IgORGA

1974 Newcastle v Nottingham Forest
https://www.youtube.com/watch?v=KHWoY-0SThs

1978 Millwall v Ipswich Town
https://www.youtube.com/watch?v=YrstfUSVtss

1982 World Cup – England v Spain
www.youtube.com/watch?v=xikswVIBgCg

1984 FA Cup Final – Everton v Watford
https://www.youtube.com/watch?v=T3o78RqGDhQ&t=6814s

1985 Luton Town v Millwall
https://www.youtube.com/watch?v=2B5670vcqIM

1985 Heysel Disaster
https://www.youtube.com/watch?v=xpy6H9t-3f0

1985 Charity Shield – Everton v Manchester United
https://www.youtube.com/watch?v=pueypxXQKr0

1986 World Cup – England v Argentina
https://www.youtube.com/watch?v=AsIWOhCXZok

1988 Simod Cup Final – Reading v Luton Town
https://www.youtube.com/watch?v=b5ZYiZpZuc4

1988 Littlewoods Cup Final – Luton Town v Arsenal
https://www.youtube.com/watch?v=At4XcJSYl04

1989 Hillsborough Disaster
https://www.youtube.com/watch?v=PYNeoTXe-SE

1990 England v West Germany
https://www.youtube.com/watch?v=vowUoccBT4E

1992 European Cup Final – Barcelona v Sampdoria
https://www.youtube.com/watch?v=UJKaqiS637M

1993 Do I Not Like That – documentary
https://www.youtube.com/watch?v=QLBA8ivsrt8

1996 England v Scotland
https://www.youtube.com/watch?v=tuzKpwmdZrA

2009 West Ham v Millwall
https://www.youtube.com/watch?v=Ma83o5WVn-4

2010 England v Germany
https://www.youtube.com/watch?v=3fMluGQDG3w

2011 West Ham v Portsmouth
https://www.youtube.com/watch?v=Vb3hbdgjCT0

2012 Aldershot v Swindon Town
https://www.youtube.com/watch?v=Yzq7qSmupgQ

2015 Brighton v Watford
https://www.youtube.com/watch?v=7sd3LtElcGg

Bibliography

Goldblatt, David, *The Ball is Round: A Global History of Football*, Viking, 2006

Sanders, Richard, *Beastly Fury: The Strange Birth of British Football*, Bantam Books, 2009

Ward, Andrew, *Football's Strangest Matches*, Portico, 2016

Acknowledgements

Thanks are due to the staff of Banbury Library and to David Kynaston, author of *Shots in the Dark: A Diary of Saturday Dreams and Strange Times*, who kindly agreed to read an early draft of *My Life on the Line*. His comments were both encouraging and very helpful. Simon Fielder also read the book in manuscript and has been a friend to the project throughout.

Thanks also to Richard Kendall, Steve Kendall and Mark Mellor for their suggestions, encouragement and enthusiasm for the idea. They helped me more than they know.

A special thanks must go to Alan Cooper who has so skilfully designed the cover and laid out the text to make this book look so good.

Lastly, special thanks go to Jacqueline, who gave me the space to work on the notes whenever I needed to and put up with all the time I spent at the laptop.

The Authors

Gavin Muge

Gavin Muge was born in Harpenden, Hertfordshire, and grew up in nearby Chiltern Green. When he was five, he began his lifelong devotion to football, watching *Match of the Day* and *The Big Match* every weekend. His first live game confirmed his undying allegiance to Luton Town FC. Although a keen schoolboy player, he realised his talents would only take him so far and he started refereeing youth matches in the Luton area at the age of 15. This led to a passion for life with a whistle and a flag. A good job in sports and leisure management allowed him to pursue a parallel career in football, and after a lot of hard work he progressed through the ranks to reach the National List of Assistant Referees in 2008. In nine seasons on the Football League line, Gavin officiated in over 250 matches, experiencing the highs and lows of the professional game. He retired from the National List in 2017, happily returning to the lower levels of non-League football, and now helps to develop the next generation of referees as a Mentor for the Bedfordshire Football Association. He has promised to deepen Simon's appreciation of the 'beautiful game', or at least teach him the Offside Law.

Simon Rae

Simon Rae tried supporting Canterbury City but switched to Liverpool FC for the 1965 FA Cup final against Leeds United. He stood in the Kop on a few occasions in the 1970s and presumably saw all the stars but cannot remember any of the football (possibly because he couldn't see any of it). He missed the one FA Cup final he was offered a ticket for (missing the train from Canterbury) and only watched the World Cup final in 1966 because rain stopped play at the county cricket match he was attending. Decades later, he brought up his son, Michael, to be a Liverpool supporter but – as he is constantly reminded – has yet to take him to Anfield. Simon's first love is cricket, and his definitive biography of W. G. Grace (1998) was praised by John Major. In addition to a second cricket book (*It's Not Cricket*), he has published six novels and several slim volumes of poetry. He presented *Poetry Please!* on BBC Radio 4 for five years and wrote satirical verse for *The Guardian* for ten years.

www.nineelmsbooks.co.uk